# ¡SALSA!

## HAVANA HEAT: BRONX BEAT

L.A.B

# ¡SALSA!

## HAVANA HEAT: BRONX BEAT

Hernando Calvo Ospina

Translator
Nick Caistor

The Latin America Bureau is an independent research and publishing organisation. It works to broaden public understanding of human rights and social and economic injustice in Latin America and the Caribbean.

First published as *Salsa: 500 jaar optimisme, liefde en ritme* by EPO, Antwerp, 1992

First published in the UK in 1995 by the Latin America Bureau (Research and Action) Ltd, 1 Amwell Street, London EC1R 1UL

A CIP catalogue record for the book is available from the British Library

ISBN 0 906156 98 X

Translator: Nick Caistor
Editor: Helen Collinson

Cover design: Andy Dark

Printed and bound by Page Bros, Norfolk NR6 6SA
Trade distribution in UK by Central Books, 99 Wallis Road, London E9 5LN
Distribution in North America by Monthly Review Press, 122 West 27th Street, New York, NY 10001

**Letters to the author:**

*From the 'Rumba Queen', Celia Cruz:*

I think your book's marvellous! I must thank you for having included me in it. I'm also deeply grateful to you for helping us to educate our audiences.

You see, even though people in Europe and elsewhere come along to our concerts, they really don't know much about the roots of this rhythm. After reading your book, they'll be so much more informed about what they're listening to...

As ever,

Celia Cruz


*From the 'Prince' of salsa, Willie Colón:*

Dear Hernando,

I was very pleased to receive your book. I'm thinking of retiring soon and I probably won't have much opportunity to write down my own version of the salsa story.

It's true what you say about salsa: it's not a type of music nor is it simply a rhythm. Salsa is a way of making music, it's a movement, a loose concept which is constantly changing...

I felt your writing showed an affinity and respect for my work. That's why I've taken the time to write these words...I wish you every success with your book....

Affectionately,

Willie Colón

# Contents

# Acknowledgements

To my parents Nabor Calvo and Elvia Ospina, to whom I owe everything.

To my daughter, Paula Andrea Calvo.

To Katlijn Declercq for her optimism and friendship.

To all Latino migrants, the true multipliers of the salsa sound.

# INTRODUCTION

## What is Salsa?

'From 1960 to around 1973, our music was in the doldrums. But when we started calling it "salsa", our young people sort of liked the name and from then on, thanks to salsa, a lot of things started to happen.'
Celia Cruz, Cuban singer

Salsa, the dictionaries tell us, means sauce or savour, condiment, flavouring; the savoury result of mixing various ingredients. Salsa is also a generic term used to describe a range of dance rhythms found in the Spanish-speaking Caribbean. It is a contemporary musical phenomenon comparable to jazz or rock.

It is also a commercial creation. When New York's Fania record company wanted to raise the profile of their salsa musicians in the early 1970s, they needed a simple, effective term which would enable people to instantly identify their product. A simple law of the market. Prior to this commercial necessity, words such as *bembé* (thick-lipped), *amor* (love), *sabor* (flavour), *fuego* (fire) and so on had often been used in the popular music of our people to signify emotional and rhythmic satisfaction.

This time, the word chosen was salsa. In fact, the word has often been heard in Caribbean musical history, some arguing that it was first used in black slave celebrations. This is hardly surprising if we recall that in the Caribbean, dancing has always been linked to social communication and to the sharing of food, which itself was often spiced up for special occasions. When in 1928 Ignacio Piñeiro used the word in his song, *'Echale Salsita'* (put a bit of sauce in it), he was using the term to imply the pleasure produced by hearing a number of instruments played and combined harmoniously. An

1

exciting, exotic 'instrumental sauce' that could help digest the hardships of daily routine.

*Salí de casa una noche aventurera*
*buscando ambiente de placer y de alegría*
*ay mi Dios, cuánto gocé!*
*En un sopor la noche pasé,*
*paseaba alegre nuestros lares luminosos*
*y llegué al bacanal.*

*En Catalina me encontré lo no pensado*
*la voz de aquél que pregonaba así:*
*'Echale salsita, échale salsita,*
*échale salsita, échale salsita.*

One night I left home in search of adventure
looking for a taste of pleasure and fun
oh my God what a time I had
I spent the night in a whirl,
left behind the lights of home
and found myself in a real party.

In Catalina I found something unexpected
a voice that cried out like this:
'put a little sauce on daddy,
put a little sauce on daddy!'

*Echale Salsita*, version by Ignacio Piñeiro

Musicians and musicologists are apt to disagree on the essence of the word, 'salsa', as these quotations reveal:

'First and foremost, the term salsa is a new invention which allows people who do not know it very well to identify a musical style. It's simply a marketing ploy.'
Ray Barreto, Puerto Rican musician

2

'Salsa is more than a type of music. It is a philosophy, an ethics, a whole way of life.'
*Libération*, Paris, 6 September 1978

'I don't like the word salsa because it's too vague, too generic. Young people today don't know about the son, the guaguancó, the danzón, the guaracha, or a mambo or rumba. To them it is all salsa.'
Cheo Feliciano, Puerto Rican singer

'In fact what they call salsa is nothing new. When Cuban music was at its height, the youngsters didn't want to know. Now they call it salsa and they think it's theirs. It's nothing more than a publicity stunt.'
Mario Bauzá, Cuban musician

'For me, salsa is the ketchup you put on French fries, or the salt and pepper on salads...'
Tito Puente, Cuban musician

'Salsa is a musical form created by the lumpen, the proletariat, the marginal.'
Fernando Ardila, Ecuadorean journalist

'Salsa is an urban form of music, the fourth created on our continent after the tango, the bossa nova and reggae.'
José Arteaga, Colombian journalist and musicologist

Whatever one thinks about the word, all are agreed that the music associated with salsa was always meant for dancing. Granddaughter of the African slave drums, daughter of Cuban *son* rhythms, about twenty years ago salsa became the expression of a whole continent, and then gradually conquered the world with its contagious, aggressive, irreverent sound.

This book offers the reader a brief, simple introduction to salsa's history and its many ramifications. At times, the story is told by imaginary bystanders so as to bring the reader that bit closer to the people and communities which created salsa. These narratives are combined with popular songs of the time.

My greatest wish is that the reader of this book should one day find him or herself dancing salsa somewhere in the world. That at first light one morning with the sweat pouring off you, and your body still full of rhythmic energy and pleasure, you will recite the salsa fanatic's prayer: 'Salsa, a blessing on you now and forever! Don't drive me wild anymore, let me rest a bit, before I have to go and earn some money. I love you for all the life you give me!'

*Mi música no queda*
*a la derecha ni a la izquierda*
*tampoco da la seña de protesta general.*
*Estoy contigo, contigo*
*y también contigo*
*para ponerte a gozar.*
*Mi música queda en el centro*
*de un tambor bien legal*


My music isn't found
To either right or left
Nor is it making any great protest.
But I'm with you, with you
with all of you
to get you to enjoy yourself.
My music's at the centre
of a sweet-sounding drum

*Mi música,* Ismael Rivera

# 1

# A CUBAN'S STORY

## Slave Drums, Spanish Songs

'And he explained that rhythm is natural, just like breathing, he would say. Everybody's got rhythm, just like everybody's got sex, and you know there are impotent men, he would say... but that doesn't mean that anyone denies the existence of sex, he would say. So nobody can deny that rhythm exists.'

Guillermo Cabrera Infante: *Three Trapped Tigers*

The history of black slaves and what they contributed to Cuban music has been passed down from mouth to mouth, song to song, generation to generation. It is in the memory of our people that this history is to be found.

We blacks arrived here because the Europeans needed strong people to work for them after they had exterminated the indigenous tribes. The genocide was so terrible that by as early as 1518 even the Spanish crown admitted that one third of the indigenous population on the American continent had been wiped out. Who can say whether this was as barbarous as the capture of some thirty to forty million black slaves from the coasts of West Africa over the following four centuries? For as long as it suited her, England was the champion of this trade, although the Dutch were the founders, since the Spanish emperor, Carlos V, had offered them a monopoly. Lacking a proper navy, Portugal acted as the intermediary between these slavetraders and the African 'petty kings'. The Sun King of France, Louis XIV, shared half of the earnings from the 'Guineas Company' set up for this purpose with his Spanish counterpart.[1]

Before my black brothers reached the coasts of the Caribbean, they had to endure four long, anguished months at sea. Many of them chose to commit suicide, hanging themselves with their chains or flinging themselves into the ocean in order to come to life again in Africa. Just as food appeals first of all to the eyes, so some of

5

these captains tried to keep their 'cargo' in a good condition, and allowed the slaves to come up on deck once a day. Sometimes this 'sunbathing' took place in the most violent storms. Even in these adverse conditions, the slaves would try and dance and sing to drown out the roaring sea and placate the supernatural forces. [2]

The slaves who had to endure this crossing, with no return ticket, were then paraded along Cuba's cobbled, steamy streets. In their heavy chains, they had to put up with the sound of pipes, the innocent noisy celebrations of children, the vulture-like gaze of possible purchasers. All of them were reduced to skin and bone, and many of the women had been raped during the journey.

That was how black people from the Yoruba or Lucumí peoples reached Cuba, to be followed by the Bantu and Congo. Other tribes were transplanted as well, but these were the most important. The Yorubas were the most advanced in their economic, social and cultural development, and this gave them a certain prestige in the eyes of their masters. But Yoruba or not, they were all forced to forget or adapt most of their own philosophy, which had sought to integrate life with death, individual endeavour with social production, personal freedom with collective norms, and leisure and pleasure with work. Forced labour and whipping meant these slaves only lasted seven years.

So we took the place of the Indians in the fields of Cuba, Indians who sadly left no trace of their music behind them. In only a few parts of the American continent can we still find instruments from this time: natural flutes, rattles, and drums made from hollowed out tree trunks like the *maguaré*.

Although the slaves had been forbidden to bring any trace of their culture with them, their continuing belief in their own religions, traditions, and musical expressions could not be chained up. Their mystery, magic and fantasy came with them from Africa. And it was through their rhythms, their singing, their music, that they spoke secretly or openly to their gods to ask for favours, to seek inspiration, to plot, or all of these at the same time. In these foreign lands they also had to adapt to the new circumstances in which they found themselves.

*Africano apareció*
*azotado con cadenas*

*su fe nunca la perdió;*
*sus manos ante la hoguera*
*se hicieron candela*
*ante el tambor.*

The African appeared
bound in chains
but never lost his faith;
his hands in the firelight
became candle flames
beating at the drum.

*Areito va a sonar*, version by Pete 'Conde' Rodríguez

By the seventeenth century, the mixed race population born in the islands was slowly increasing. Meanwhile there were changes in the political economy of Spain and its colonies which led to the growth of agriculture and trade. As a result, a larger labour force was required, and more slaves were sent for. The increasing numbers of blacks prompted their masters to create social structures through which to control them. If the slaves remained scattered, they were harder to keep an eye on, and did not work as hard. It is worth noting that there had been slave uprisings from as early as 1522. [3]

## African influences

So the black slaves were organised into societies or associations, based on the different African nations they belonged to. Ironically, it was within these groupings that their ancestral rites and religious beliefs could be preserved. Here, too, new percussion instruments were created.

One African custom which changed very little was the playing of sacred drum beats. 'If we wish to find a symbol that embraces the cultural identity of the Africans brought to Cuba by the slave trade' wrote Leonardo Acosta, 'and which has been able to represent that identity throughout four centuries of resistance despite the most inhuman and alienating conditions known in history, that symbol would be the drum.'

7

   The skin of these sacred, ritual drums could not be stretched using heat, because they contained a specific power, a sort of divinity, which was able to bring order, to call for things, to speak. They guarded their secret jealously, and it was known only to the man who built them, following all the rites that wood had to pass through if it were to become the body of a sacred drum. In Yoruba worship, Iyá is the name given to the most important drum, the next largest is called Itótele, and the smallest Okónkolo. Talent and inspiration are natural gifts which should be respected and appreciated. There is also a hierarchy among drummers, because not all of them have the same *ashé*, the power needed if the drumbeats are to be heard by the gods. And every god has his special song.

## SONG FOR CHANGO

Solo:    *Changó motí awá.*
Chorus:  *Ea.*
Solo:    *Aladdó mití awá.*
Chorus:  *Ea.*
Solo:    *Obbá odo aladdó,*
          *Changó mití awá.*
Chorus:  *Ea.*
Solo:    *Alá molé bi.*
Chorus:  *Ea.*
Solo:    *Eñí la mo do la koka.*
Chorus:  *Ea.*
Solo:    *Addeún elesha.*
Chorus:  *Ea.*

## SONG FOR OBATALA

Solo:    *Babá fururu eró ereó*
          *ocañeñe elellibbó*
          *elé erí ifá*
          *batí basabwo*
          *ellibó 'rere batibaó*

*enú aye ya aggwaró*
*eyá awá 'roró*
*elese okán*

Chorus: repeats the same

Solo: *Babá elese okán*
*babá elese okán.*

Chorus: *Eyá awá 'roró*
*elese okán.*

But these chants were only part of the picture. Who has ever seen a black person who does not dance when he sings? The music was extrovert, guaranteed to make people get up and dance. If in Africa even the gods danced, they were going to do the same in Cuba. Here's a story from the Yoruba tradition which has been handed down to our own day. Once upon a time, only Orunlá, the oldest and most powerful of the African divinities, had the right to dance and to be the 'owner of the drum'. Changó, the god of virility, was so jealous of this that he made a deal with him. Changó was given the power of music, total euphoria, in exchange for letting Orunla have knowledge. The young Changó took the drum and the gift of dancing, and in return gave Orunla the board of Ifa, which held the power of knowing all that was hidden in past, present, and future. [5]

Before going any further, let us look at the important role that *santería* played in this process. It is well-known that the Catholic church increased its influence by instilling fear into anyone who practised rites contrary to its teachings. That is why the African slave cults had to be kept secret for so many years, since they were seen as pagan rituals, inspired by Satan or more earthly powers. But such was the black people's need to maintain their own traditions that they managed to conceal them within the complicated rites of the Catholic church, allying the Christian saints with the stones, shells, iron and other objects their own gods inhabited. It is from this mingling of rites – above all the ones brought by the Yoruba people – with those of the Catholic church, that the term *santería* was born. And there can be no doubt that if the black people had not so cleverly adapted to the circumstances they found themselves in, their songs and dances would not have survived.

9

*Cuando siento los tambores africanos*
*con su ritmo misterioso de Arará*
*hierve el eco de la sangre de mis venas*
*y a mi Santo una oración quiero cantar.*

*Santa Bárbara que escuchas desde el cielo*
*oye el ruego de esta mística oración*
*dame siempre, papá mío, tu consuelo*
*y salud para alegrar mi corazón.*

When I hear the African drums
with their mysterious Arará rhythm
they echo in the hot blood of my veins
and make me want to sing to my Saint.

Santa Barbara listening in heaven
hear the plea of this mystic prayer
give me forever your consolation, Father,
and health to gladden my heart.

*Tambores africanos*, version by Celina and Reutilio

There were Yoruba songs addressed to the divinities, in other words sacred songs; but there were others which simply told a tale, and still more that were satirical, or gibes and challenges to people present. The most important part of this kind of song was the narrator's ability to improvise. It was the Congo people who from the eighteenth century onwards were renowned for their prowess in this difficult art.

*Han sonado los tambores en el barracón*
*y en el canto de los congos hay una oración*
*implorándole a Changó y a Yemayá*
*que le traigan a sus hijos la felicidad.*

*Ya Francisco se prepara para consultar,*
*y le pide al Padre Sambia que con su poder*
*le traiga fuerza y luz para vencer*
*en la tierra toda dificultad.*

The drums are beating in the slave huts
the Congo people are singing a song of prayer
calling on Chango and Yemaya
to make their children happy

Francisco is making ready to consult the gods
asking Father Sambia to use his power
to bring him the strength and light
to overcome all hardships on this earth.

*A Francisco*, version by Celina and Reutilio

The two kinds of songs shared exactly the same structure, alternating solo and chorus. The singer or narrator had to have great musical and poetic talent to develop his theme as the song progressed. Any event from the past or present in the slave community could be used. It was the singer's ability to improvise rather than the beauty of his voice which counted most. The chorus responded in a dialogue with the single voice.[5] But this pattern was also open to improvisation: sometimes there were dialogues between two singers and two choruses, or between singer and instruments; or even between the instruments themselves. The most important thing in all this was the spirit of constant renewal and innovation, born of the state of mind of both the individual and the group; a state of mind which has always produced in us a feeling of intoxication, eventually subsiding into a sense of bodily and spiritual ease.

This pattern of dialogue gave rise to a tradition which still survives today: that of calling the instruments male or female when they are paired together: so the maracas are female, the bongos male, and so on. The instruments are treated as if they really did have their own sex: female instruments are the ones that sound higher, the males have a deeper sound.[6] And not only do they have a body, they have a soul too: all true musicians of today know how to look after their instruments, just as their African ancestors gave them food, made sure they rested, enjoyed themselves, and kept them from suffering.

Another key aspect of our African heritage is our ability to dance to any music. It does not matter if the music is to express pleasure, love, grief or hatred; it makes no difference whether it is to summon prosperity and ward off misfortune, or simply to pass the time. All these different kinds of music produced – just as they do today –

ways of dancing which gradually changed and modified to become more complex. Often, this dancing was prohibited because it was seen as idolatrous or because it kept people from working.[7] There is nothing really surprising in this, as history is full of similiar prohibitions which sooner or later bow to the creative forces they contain, and legalise what they had previously banned.

I may have made the slaves' experiences sound like a happy story. The reality was harsh. This music and its songs, the dances and trances and collective frenzy were all safety valves, miraculous cures for the dispossessed. The long, hard days in the sugar, tobacco or coffee plantations left only a few hours of leisure, which were seized upon to bring some enjoyment to the short life offered them.

> *Déjalo que duerma hasta mañana*
> *que la campanada le ordenará*
> *ir al trabajo en hora temprana*
> *o el látigo fiero lo llevará,*
> *y así van los negros*
> *muy temprano pa'l batey.*
> *(coro)*
> *laborando, siempre laborando.*
>
> Let him sleep until the morning
> the bell will soon be telling him
> he must get to work at sunup
> or the fierce whip will force him there
> so we black people have to go
> at first light to the sugar mill.
> (chorus)
> Working, always working.
>
> *En el ingenio*, version by Trío Matamoros

From black Africa we inherited a philosophy of life, death and community expressed through rhythm and multiple rhythms, improvisation, and dance. Their hands gave birth to all kinds of percussion instruments which have now become universal.

## European influences

The European colonisers of our American lands made important contributions to our Cuban culture too. Chief among them was the imposition of their language, made all the easier by the diverse number of African languages amongst Cuba's slave population. The Spaniards brought with them not only their love of romance, but also their folklore of rhymes, songs, stories, and, of course, their musical instruments.

Europe could boast a wide range of instruments: trumpets, cornets, trombones, violins, double basses, flutes, clarinets and many more. Not forgetting the mandola (an early form of mandolin), harp, accordeon, and the essential guitar, to which we took away or added strings to make our Cuban 'tres', the Puerto Rican 'cuatro', the Colombian 'tiple' guitar, or the Mexican big guitar. [8] In those days, Europe lagged behind Africa when it came to rhythm and percussion: so much so that Beethoven met with disapproval when he introduced drums into his Seventh Symphony. What were extraordinarily developed in European music were melody, harmony and musical composition.

So it was that the blacks, the Europeans, and those born in Cuba gradually brought into existence what the Cuban musical researcher Fernando Ortiz has called the 'creole symphony', an expression of our national musical identity. Together they created that 'flavour', that *sandunga* so typically Cuban and Caribbean. Sandunga is a word which comes from *sa*, or salt cellar in Andalucian, and *ndungu*, or black African pepper. Salt and pepper, then, are the twin symbols of Cuban music.

To see how these different elements fused to form our Cuban musical identity, we must go back to the Cuban countryside in the eighteenth century. Since the late seventeenth century, poor Spanish migrants had settled in Cuba, bringing with them the rich tradition of the Spanish couplet. This was an ancient form of singing, with both rhymes and verses, that owed a lot to the Arabs. In this new land, with its different social conditions, the sung couplet underwent a series of transformations, especially when the black slaves made it their own. The way the 'tres' guitar came into being clearly shows an African-Spanish fusion. [9]

From the eighteenth century onwards, events in the countryside were described in music, to the accompaniment of a mandola, while the typical dance became a series of stamps and jumps. This kind of country singing, known as *guajira*, was quite different from urban music. As with almost all peasant repertoire, the *guajira* was a very simple musical form, drawn directly from Spanish roots. When their masters went out visiting, it was common for the blacks in charge of their carriages to improvise a dance, singing rhymes and accompanying themselves on the tiple guitar.

> *Soy la linda melodía*
> *que en el campestre retiro*
> *siempre le llevó al guajiro*
> *la esperanza y la alegría*
>
> *En noches de romería*
> *inspiro a los trovadores;*
> *cantantes y bailadores*
> *gozan con el zapateo*
> *y se olvidan de morfeo*
> *para tributarme honores...*

I am the sweet song
which in the secluded countryside
can always bring the labourers
hope and happiness

During nights of celebration
I inspire the poets;
Singers and dancers
enjoy their merry dance
They forsake the arms of Morpheus
to render me homage.

*Yo soy el punto cubano*, version by Celina and Reutilio

It is time to mention an event outside Cuba in the late eighteenth century which had a profound effect on its musical traditions. In 1791 a revolution against French colonial rule broke out in Haiti, the producer of the world's finest sugar. Some of the French, the Creoles and a few blacks fled from Haiti to Cuba. Concurrently, the crisis which this rebellion provoked in Haiti's sugar exports enabled

Cuba to take the lead, which in turn brought about a gradual migration from the Cuban countryside to the ports dispatching the sugar. In this way, the music and dance of the countryside began to seep into Cuba's towns.

*La zafra ya comenzó*
*negro afila tu machete*
*enyuga tu buey y vete*
*a trabajar bajo el sol;*
*ve cantando una canción*
*para que no te amedrentes.*
*Al sudor métele el diente*
*para que te bendiga Dios.*
*Trabajas de sol a sol*
*para ganarte la comida*
*y cuando se acaba el día*
*vuelves de nuevo al bohío;*
*y te duele el cuerpo entero*
*por lo mucho que has sufrido,*
*y ese callo majadero*
*te mantuvo en agonía;*
*pero tú sigues cantando*
*la canción del carretero*
*que se oye de día a día*
*allá por la serranía:*
*(coro)*
*Hecha pa'lante mi buey*
*que tenemos que avanzar,*
*hoy vamo' a dar veinte viajes de caña*
*pa' la central, oh, oh, oh.*

The sugar harvest has begun
sharpen your machete
hitch up your ox and go
work under the burning sun;
go singing a song
to keep your spirits up.
give it all you've got
to gain God's blessing.
You work from dawn to dusk

to earn your daily bread
and when the day is done
go back to your slave's hut;
your whole body is aching
from all you have suffered
and that damn foot callus
kept you in agony all day;
yet you go on singing
the ox-driver's song
heard day after day
up in the hills:

(chorus)
Come on there my oxen
we have to get on
today we've twenty loads of sugar
to take to the mill, oh, oh, oh.

*La zafra*, version by Ricardo Ray and his orchestra

As well as those who fled to Cuba from Haiti, a considerable number also arrived from French Louisiana when Napoleon sold the territory in 1820. This strengthened the cultural contacts with France, whose fashions in dress, singing and dancing were copied by the local bourgeoisie. Meanwhile, the blacks from Haiti brought with them a kind of festivity known as French *tumbas*. The word tumba meant a group or collection of people and the dances performed at these tumbas were very similar to those of the French salons.[10]

From this period onwards, thanks mainly to French influences, various elements of Western European music were incorporated into the Cuban people's own repertory. Examples of this are the minuet, the pavane, the polka, the mazurka. French romances, operatic arias, and the waltz also helped create other rhythmic possibilities such as the bolero.

By 1794 the newspaper *Papel Periódico de la Habana* mentions the popularity in Cuban towns of European-style dances or square dances like the *contredanse*. It is thought the contredanse was first brought to Cuba by the English officers who took Havana in 1762. Although they had become fashionable in the salons of London and

Paris, these square dances were based on the country dancing of Normandy peasants. [11] By the early nineteenth century, a specifically Cuban form of contredanse had become the rage not only in Havana's academies and dancing salons, but also in the 'cuna' dances in Havana's poor neighbourhoods. Young men from high society came to these 'cuna dances' to fraternise with mulatta women, the true experts in these rhythms. Some of the high class houses organised dances with tickets sold in advance, and advertised them in the *Papel Periódico de la Habana*. One such advert states: 'To all ticket holders: today, Sunday the 9th, dances in celebration of Our Catholic Queen (God Protect Her) will start at the house of the deceased Doña Felipa Rodríguez at eight o'clock sharp'. [12]

This dancing boom brought with it a great demand for musicians, and a number of orchestras were formed. New instruments from Europe such as the clarinet, the flute, the violin, and the trombone were adopted, while the guitar, the mandola and the tiple guitar had already been assimilated. Gradually the musicians started to lengthen the tunes of the contredanses by repeating parts of them and introducing their own variations. The enchanted dancers would then throw money at the orchestra to keep the tune going for as long as possible. Although by no means common practice, some orchestras brought in black musicians who added their own cultural touch to the contredanse.

It was around this time that the orchestras started to become more clearly defined. Two kinds of musical group existed in the towns. The first was known as a 'traditional' orchestra or group and usually included a clarinet, cornet, trombone, two violins, two small or kettle drums, and the *güiro* (made from a gourd). The other, promoted by foreigners – mostly French – was based on the piano and the flute, and was very common in bourgeois homes and elegant salons, where café-concerts were held. Added to the piano and flute were two violins, a double-bass, a pair of side drums, and another percussion instrument.

Meanwhile, various kinds of dancing from the outlying rural areas continued to permeate Cuba's emerging national music. One such country dance was the *danzón*, or big dance, which came directly from the ancient dances in Matanzas, in the east of Cuba. [13] In 1879, Miguel Faílde and his Traditional Group created the first danzón, '*La altura del Simpsón*'. Over the coming years, the danzón was the main dance in Cuba and remained popular until the 1920s. Its gentle rhythms even started to infiltrate the dance halls of Europe and the United States, where it was danced to classical European music. The rhythm of the danzón did not permit any variations by the musicians, who had to keep strictly to the arrangements on their music-sheets, giving the danzón an almost classical veneer. But the danzón's popularity did not exclude the rise of other dance forms. By the late nineteenth century, Cuban towns had become immersed in the songs and dances of the surrounding countryside. These were played alongside the contredanse, the danzón, and other more classical kinds of music.

> *Por carretera central*
> *me voy pa' la capital,*
> *el guajiro aquí*
> *lucha por un ideal*
> *sueña con un porvenir*
> *por eso quiere vivir en la capital.*

> I'm setting off down the highroad
> on my way to the capital,
> the peasants here
> are fighting for an ideal
> dreaming of a future
> that's why they want to live in the capital.

*Pa' la capital*, version by Guillermo Portabales

# 2
# WAITING FOR CASTRO
## Son, Jazz and Chachacha

'With our music we Cubans have exported more dreams and
pleasures than with our tobacco, more sweetness and energy than
with all our sugar. Afro-Cuban music is fire, savour, and smoke; it
is syrup, charm and relief. It is like a sonorous rum, which brings
people together and makes them treat each other as equals. It brings
the senses to dynamic life.'
Fernando Ortíz. *La africanía en la música folklórica de Cuba.*

Few would argue that the 1959 revolution was the watershed
between two distinct phases in twentieth century Cuban music. This
chapter will give a brief overview of what happened up until the
revolution. Going back to the turn of the century, we have to
remember that what were grandly called cities in Cuba were actually
little more than large towns, still largely untouched by
industrialisation. The salons and private parties in the centre of these
towns were contredanse and danzón territory, while in the poor
neighbourhoods on the outskirts, street dances known as rumbas
were all the rage. The instruments played at these street parties
included conga drums, often accompanied by wooden fish-packing
boxes or other such makeshift instruments.

Cuba's ten-year war of independence against Spanish colonial
rule (1868-78) destroyed the sugar industry but contributed to the
abolition of slavery in 1886. This meant that while the blacks won
freedom of movement, they were not free from poverty, as the slump
in sugar production created high rural unemployment. It was this
combination of factors which prompted not only thousands of former
slaves, but also creoles and mulattos to migrate to the towns, taking
their cultural traditions with them.

*Qué es lo que pasa en mi Cuba (solo)*
     *sí señor (coro)*
*que ya no se vende caña*
     *como no*
*yo me valdré de mi maña*
     *sí señor*
*para que su precio suba*
     *como no...*

*Qué le pasa al 'buen vecino',*
     *sí señor*
*que está tramando con saña,*
     *como no*
*por un precio muy mezquino,*
     *sí señor*
*quiere comer mucha caña*
     *como no...*

What is happening in this Cuba of mine
     (Chorus): Oh, yes, sir
no sugar's being sold any more
     That's right
but I've got the knack
     oh, yes, sir
of getting the price raised
     that's right...

What is happening to the 'good neighbour',
     oh, yes, sir
he's behaving very badly
     that's right
he wants to pay next to nothing
     oh, yes, sir
and eat a lot of sugar
     that's right

*El buen vecino*, version by Lorenzo Hierrezuelo

One of these traditions was the *guajira*, a sound directly influenced by Spanish song. It was in the guajira that the Cuban aristocracy saw their chance to wipe out all traces of the days of slavery, and 'vulgar', black music. *'Guajirismo'* was to drown out all else. At the same time, the playing of drums in public places was banned. In response, groups in the Cuban capital, including some blacks and mulattos, took up guitars and lutes, dressed up in loose-fitting *guayabera* shirts and palm hats from the countryside, stuck a machete in their waistband and began to imitate peasant songs. The tunes were mostly about an imaginary countryside where peasants lived in poverty but were happy and cheerful.[1] Inevitably, this guajira music became socially acceptable, alongside the contredanse and the danzón.

## The rise of *son*

Everything was going to plan for the Cuban bourgeoisie when a fly buzzed into the ointment. A new sound arrived from the east of the island, the region where the black influence was strongest, where revolts against the Spaniards had started, and where Castro's guerrilla army would later be based. This sound was so unique that it changed the whole direction of Cuban music. It was to influence the subsequent development of dance music not only in Cuba and the Caribbean, but across the whole continent. It was the *son*.

Cuban historians such as Alejo Carpentier trace the son back to a few decades after the arrival of the Spaniards, and the joyful songs of the black woman Teodora Ginez, a native of Baracoa in the east of Cuba. More recently, in the nineteenth century, so-called *'bungas'* started to appear in the black, rural areas of Santiago, Bayamo, Manzanillo, Guantánamo, Guanabacoa and Baracoa. Originally, these were clay pots in which oil was carried; they were turned into musical instruments by making a hole in the side, which was blown into to make sounds. Later the same word was applied to musical groups comprising a guitar, a tres, maracas, claves, and the bongo, with its high-pitched sound and its air of magic ritual. As time went by, the botijuela or the marimbula, the African hand piano, was added to the ensemble. These groups formed a perfect balance between Spanish and African elements, and gave rise to the basic structure of what came to identify Cuban music: the son. And it was

The fusion of Spanish and African influences was encapsulated in the basic format of the son: a story known as a *'motivo'* and told by a solo singer, a collective affirmation in the chorus combined with the dynamic power of the instruments. The son offered its public a mocking, irreverent message, which appealed to the poorer sectors of society and gradually became their anthem. The son was both song and dance; the simple dance was performed by a couple in a style not seen before.[2]

*Valga que hablé pues si no*
*me coge el gallo 'e Rufina.*
*Eso lo dijo un perico*
*porque un gallo equivoca'o*
*le confundió con gallina.*

*Lo corrió por la guardarraya*
*y el periquito cansao'*
*en el suelo se tiró, ay dios,*
*y cuando el gallo llegó*
*quiso enseguida jugar.*
*Como un tiro el perico,*
*del suelo se levantó*
*y al gallo le dijo así:*

*Cuidadito compay gallo, cuidadito,*
*cuidadito compay gallo, cuidadito,*
*cuidadito compay gallo, cuidadito.*

*Aquí donde usted me ve*
*yo tengo mi periquita,*
*busque Ud su gallinita*
*esas sí son para Ud.*

*Cuidadito compay gallo, cuidadito...*

*Cuando el periquito vió*
*que la cosa iba de veras,*
*al gallo le dijo, espera!*
*ay, usted se equivocó.*

*Esa gracia compay gallo*
*no me acaba de gustar...*

Just as well I can speak because if not
I'd have been had by Rufina's rooster
so said a parakeet one day
after a confused rooster
had mistaken him for a hen.

all round the fence it chased him
until the weary parakeet
collapsed onto the ground my god,
when the rooster came up
it wanted to start the action straightaway
but like a shot the parrakeet
raised itself from the floor
and told that rooster

watch what you're doing, rooster friend
watch what you're doing, rooster friend
watch what you're doing, rooster friend

It may not look like it to you
but I've got a lady wife at home
you go look for a nice little hen
they're the ones for you.

watch what you're doing, rooster friend...

when the parrakeet saw
that things were getting serious
he shouted to the rooster Wait!
it's a big mistake you're making
your charms my rooster friend
are not my thing at all...

*Compay gallo*, version by Ñico Saquito

The son musicians were mainly peasants or workers who did not
know the first thing about musical annotation. Their gifts and

23

inspiration were natural: they learned by ear. They practised during work breaks, at weekends in someone's house, or in their backyards. As often as not they made their own rudimentary instruments.

It was shortly before the First World War that the son first tried to establish itself in Havana. It came with the mass of country people we mentioned earlier, as well as those who came after every sugar harvest, and those out of work between harvests. The creation of a new standing army which young lads were pressganged to join, prompted many musicians to leave the countryside and try out their musical talents in the cities.

There the '*soneros*' started playing at popular and religious celebrations. As they went round, they asked for money to help balance their family budgets. All of them had day jobs, as no one could think of living from music alone. It was only on Easter Saturday or New Year's Eve that they could hope to earn a decent amount, although there was always the risk they would get nothing, since the contracts they made were always verbal. If the person holding the celebration refused to pay, there was no point in going to the police: they were usually on the side of the debtor, and all the musicians got were maltreatment and insults. [3]

The impact of the son was so great that it began to have repercussions on other musical forms. In 1910, for example, the great musician José Urfé composed '*El bombín de Barreto*' in an attempt to update the danzón. To do so, he added a son theme in the second part and at the end, so creating the *danzonete*. From that moment on, the danzonete became a semi-clandestine method by which the son could spread its influence. Undeterred, the Cuban bourgeoisie continued to try and stop the growth of this new sound from the eastern end of the island.

Because of its origins on the margins of society and its extraordinary popularity among the working people, the son was violently rejected in the elegant salons of the Cuban aristocracy, who succeeded in having the government ban it. The main reason alleged was the obscenity and immorality of the movements it provoked in those who danced it. A Cienfuegos newspaper reported on 31 May 1917: 'The police led away a group of women who were dancing the son in a scandalous manner at no.50 Arango Street'. But by 1918 in the same city, it was being danced in 'high society' at the Yacht Club ball. [4]

Like damned up water, the son finally burst through all obstacles. So potent was this music that by 1920 the ban was lifted, and its music, which had already triumphed throughout the countryside, took the carnival dances of that year by storm. Groups such as the Estudiantina Oriental, the Sexteto Habanero, or the Sexteto Occidente led by María Teresa Vera put an end to the discrimination against the new sound.

There is no doubt that the son's massive popularity owed much to the people's poet, Nicolás Guillén, the musician, Miguel Matamoros, and Ignacio Piñeiro, former bassist with the Sexteto de Occidente, founder of the Sexteto Nacional, and author of almost 350 compositions. Their exciting, original arrangements and combinations ensured that the son spread not only throughout Cuba but to many other parts of the world.

Havana was now filled with son groups. Because of its poor sonority, the marímbula was replaced with the double bass and some groups even included a vertical pianini and a trumpet. Arsenio Rodríguez, a tres player who became blind at the age of thirteen, revised the original septet format for a much larger group. In the late 1930s, he added the tumbadora, which until then had not been used at all in the son, and added a brass section made up of two or three trumpets. Many of the groups which adopted this line-up continued to call themselves septets or '*sonoras*'.

> *Dicen que de Cuba bella*
> *es originario el son*
> *tierra de café y tabaco,*
> *y tiene sabor a ron.*
>
> *Qué ritmo más rico tiene el son,*
> *alegre y cubano pa' bailar.*
>
> *Dicen que la ma' Teodora*
> *fue fundadora del son,*
> *ella es merecedora*
> *de la vivencia del son.*
>
> *Qué ritmo más rico tiene el son...*
>
> *Si vienes del extranjero*

*y tú lo qiueres bailar,*
*lleva el ritmo de las claves,*
*marca el compás del bongó*
*y verás como te sabe,*
*qué rico y qué bueno el son...*


They say that lovely Cuba
is the birthplace of the son
a land of coffee and tobacco
with the sweet taste of rum.

Listen to the beautiful rhythm of the son
so lively and Cuban to dance to

They say that old ma' Teodora
was the creator of the son
she's the one to praise
for bringing the son to life.

Listen to the beautiful rhythm of the son...

If you're coming from abroad
and you want to dance the son
listen to the rhythm of the claves
listen to the bongo beat
and you'll see how sweet it is
how wonderful is the son...

*Sin clave y bongó no hay son*, version by Orquesta Aragón


   As time went by, neither the emerging capitalism on the island
nor the US companies could resist taking advantage of this new
phenomenon. The arrival of fragile records played on wind-up
gramophones opened up a whole new market for them. The spread
of radio made the music business even more lucrative. In those early
days, when musicians were given the chance to do a radio broadcast,
they had to cluster round a single microphone for all their instruments
to be heard. But these radio programmes were a mixed blessing. On
the one hand, they encouraged the spread of the son, on the other

they limited their musical potential by reducing songs to a few short phrases.

By the 1930s, son rhythms were influencing all kinds of Cuban songs, and were encouraging various rhythmic hybrids: the *bolero-son*, the *guaracha-son*, and the *guajira-son*. The first guajira-son was composed by the workman Joseíto Fernández, who called it 'Guajira Guantanamera', now famous the world over. This lengthy tale used simple quotations from José Martí, the hero of Cuban independence, which could be changed at will with each performance. For 18 years, Joseíto had a radio programme in which the news items were sung for the audience in verses that followed the rhythm of the Guantánamera. This song showed most clearly to the whole world what Cuba could make of the Spanish romantic tradition.

After the Second World War, great strides were made in television, radio, and cinema production. As a consequence, tourism grew in Cuba, and this brought with it an immense, though largely hidden, market for prostitution. Private companies also supplied every kind of entertainment required by their patrons. New musicians met the demand in hotels, cabarets and dance halls. Some of these new groups were female, such as the Anacaona, Ensueño and Orbe; female performers like Celeste Mendoza, Paulina Alvarez (who in the 1930s had been known as the 'empress of the danzonete'), Rita Montaner, and the singer Celia Cruz – still going strong today – featured in the luxury hotels as exotic attractions.

*Oye ya, oye ya,*
*oye ya a mí bongó resonar,*
*oye ya, oye ya,*
*oye ya a mi bongó resonar.*

*A mí me dicen la negra*
*porque sueno mi bongó*
*y hay muchas que no son negras*
*pero que suenan como yo*

*Oye ya, oye ya...*

*A mí me gusta la rumba*
*porque es un baile moral,*

27

*depende del movimiento*
*que se le ponga al bailar*

*oye ya, oye ya, oye ya...*

*Me gusta cantar guaracha*
*también canto guaguancó,*
*pero si siento una rumba*
*no hay quien cante como yo...*

(chorus)
Listen, just listen
listen to my bongo beat.
Listen, just listen,
listen to my bongo beat.

(soloist)
they call me the black woman
because of the way I play my bongo
but you don't have to be black
to play it like I do

Listen, just listen...

I like the rumba
because it's a moral dance
it depends on how you move

when you come to dance it

Listen, just listen...

I like to sing guaracha
and I sing guaguanco as well,
but if I hear a rumba
there's no-one sings like me...

*Oye ya*, version by Miguel Matamoros and his Cuarteto Maisí

Towards the end of the 1920s, when the Trío Matamoros were all the rage in Cuba, a group from the town of Matanzas arrived on the scene, named at first the Estudiantina Matancera, later known throughout the continent as the Sonora Matancera. Their career began on Radio Progreso where they earned a dollar a time: this was divided equally among the nine musicians, with a tenth part set aside to cover administrative costs. When the Puerto Rican singer Daniel Santos joined them as a regular singer in 1939, Sonora Matancera hit the big time, each of them now earning $1.20 each in a radio programme sponsored by a brewery. Celia Cruz later teamed up with this versatile man – in fact, some fifty different singers have appeared with the group – and today Sonora Matancera is a legend in Cuban music. [5]

## From Jazz to Chachacha

Before going any further, we ought to mention the main external influence on Cuban music in the years between the world wars. Black jazz bands from the United States first began to arrive on the island in the 1920s. As we have seen, Cuban music and musicians have always had a knack for taking up new sounds and by the middle of the decade there were jazz bands in Cuba made up entirely of Cubans. Traditional rhythms like the son, the guaracha, rumba, danzón and so on were played by these huge orchestras too, producing a number of stars, such as the clarinettist, Mario Bauzá, and providing a constant output of music for the tourist trade.

These home-grown jazz bands, whose heyday was in the 1940s, incorporated instruments from the smaller groups. The piano, played in the Cuban style, was accompanied by the doublebass, drums, four or five saxophones, three or four trumpets, a trombone. The percussion section was almost entirely Cuban: tumbadora, bongo and timbal drums; the maracas and the güiro. This line-up was very similar to the one created by a Cuban living in Mexico by the name of Pérez Prado, who was the first person to adapt North American jazz bands to Cuban traditions.

In these years, Cuban music underwent a series of changes that made it more cosmopolitan. For example, the traditional Cuban bolero became slower, more passionate, with dissonant chords. The name by which this new way of singing became known revealed its origins: '*cantar con feeling*' (sing with feeling). The bolero in Mexico and Puerto Rico experienced a similar transformation.

The charanga groups (based on flute and violins) were also revived at this time. José Urfé and Cheo Belén Puig were its main innovators: as I have already said, Urfé changed the form of the danzón by including a sung section. In the 1940s however, the danzón went back to its original instrumental form which, absorbing other rhythmic combinations, led to the fabulous, world-famous mambo. In 1948, a young violinist who played in a Havana club called the '*Prado y Neptuno*' composed a tune known as '*Engañadora*' (The Cheat). Enrique Jorrín for his part had added a final section to his danzón music when the instrumentalists played a *montuno*. Jorrín himself has said that the name of this new rhythm was suggested by the sound that the dancers made with their feet as they danced: chachacha... So '*Engañadora*' became the first chachacha ever played. It was recorded in 1953 and the reaction was instantaneous. Suddenly, everyone wanted to dance the new dance.

*A Prado y Neptuno*
*iba una chiquita*
*que todos los hombres*
*la tenían que mirar.*

*Estaba gordita*
*muy bien formadita*
*era graciosita*
*y en resumen colosal.*

*Pero todo en esta vida*
*se sabe sin siquiera averiguar,*
*se ha sabido que en sus formas*
*rellenos tan sólo hay.*

*Hay qué bobas son las mujeres*
*que nos tratan de engañar...*

*Ya nadie la mira,*
*ya nadie suspira,*
*ya sus almohaditas*

*nadie las quiere apreciar.*

To the Prado y Neptuno
a young girl used to go
she had all the men
staring at her charms.

She was plump
in all the right places
she was full of fun
nothing short of sensational.

But in this life everything
gets found out without trying
soon everyone knew her shape
was only due to padding.

How silly women are
when they try to cheat on us...

Nobody looks at her now
nobody sighs after her,
her shapely cushions
don't interest anyone at all.

*Engañadora*, version by Enrique Jorrín and his Orquesta
América

Perhaps the best chachacha group was the Orquesta Aragón.[6]
Orestes Aragón Cantero founded the orchestra in 1939 and led the
group until 1948, when he had to step down due to a lung disease,
although in fact he died of a heart attack in 1963. From the 1930s
onwards, many Cuban musicians died of lung problems because of
their poor diet and excess of work. Often they played all night,
without even a coffee break, earning as little as 25 cents. After
Orestes had left the orchestra, Rafael Lay took charge. Lay had
joined the group as a violinist at the age of 12. In those days, the
other musicians used to have to wake the young boy up, because he
kept falling asleep and the dancing was supposed to go on until four

31

in the morning.[7] Lay, who died tragically in 1982, became the symbol of Cuban music after the death of Beny Moré.

During one of many nights out on the town, the musician and chauffeur Miguel Matamoros met a tall black man who wore a broad-brim hat and carried a cane. This was Beny Moré, the man who was to make jazz bands completely Cuban. Beny had learnt to play the guitar in his childhood so as to earn a few pesos at parties in his neighbourhood. Later, he started playing in bars, streets, and parks across Havana. It was in these inauspicious places that he learnt his highpitched tonalities and the sudden changes of register that were to make him famous. In 1945, Matamoros, who had formed a group intended to rival the jazz bands, took Beny with him to Mexico. Both of them were spontaneous, intuitive musicians who could not read music but were amazingly creative.

In Mexico, Beny met Pérez Prado, who was rapidly becoming the king of mambo. Together they made several recordings and films. On his return to Cuba, now full of clubs, cabarets, and gringos, Beny started his own big band, which he called 'my tribe'. He used to demonstrate all the arrangements for the different instruments with his own voice, imitating the sound of each one. Beny Moré, the 'wild man of rhythm', the 'aristocrat of Cuban popular song' bewildered many people as his tall frame swayed and his cane became the sceptre of his kingdom: the kingdom of rhythm. [8]

*Perdón vida de mi vida*
*perdón si te he faltado*
*perdón cariñito amado*
*ángel dorado, dame tu perdón...*

*Si tú sabes que te quiero*
*con todo el corazón,*
*que tú eres el anhelo*
*y mi única ilusión,*
*ven calma mi sufrir*
*con un poco de amor,*
*que es todo lo que ansía*
*mi pobre corazón.*

Forgive me life of my life
forgive me if I've let you down
forgive me, my lovely little one
my golden angel, forgive me...

You know I love you
with all my heart,
that you are all I want
my only hope in life
come and calm my suffering
with a little of your love,
that is the only desire
of this poor heart of mine.

Perdón, version by Beny Moré with the Mexican Pedro
Vargas

When Fidel Castro and his guerrilla army entered Havana in 1959,
some Cuban musicians left for Mexico or the United States. Many
more stayed: Félix Chapottín, Pacho Alonso, the Septeto Nacional,
Bebo Valdez, Arcaño y sus Maravillas, Tata Güinez, the Matamoros,
the Orquesta Aragón... Beny Moré was amongst those who
adamantly refused to leave. 'Nobody's going to make me leave
Cuba,' he used to say. 'I'm not bothered about dollars, what I like is
to be able to walk down the street and hear the ordinary people say:
'Hey, wild man, how's it going?' And I reply: 'this is my flesh and
blood.'[9] So spoke the greatest son musician of all time.

*Aquí pensaban seguir*
*ganando el ciento por ciento,*
*con casas y apartamentos*
*y echar el pueblo a sufrir;*
*y seguir de modo cruel*
*contra el pueblo conspirando*
*para seguirlo explotando*
*y en eso llegó Fidel.*

*(coro)*
*y se acabó la diversión,*
*llegó el comandante y mandó a parar...*

They thought they could go on
earning a hundred per cent
with their houses and their flats
making the people suffer;
go on in their cruel way
plotting against the people
so they could exploit them more
but then Fidel arrived.

(Chorus)
The fun is over,
the comandante arrived and ordered it to stop...

*Y en eso llegó Fidel*, version by Carlos Puebla

# 3

# NEW YORK, NEW YORK

## A Puerto Rican's Story

'My name: Tito Rodríguez, singer and leader of this orchestra.
The musicians call me the boss, the voice, and other names I can't
repeat to you...' With his hair cut short 'like real men have it' and
an impeccable tuxedo – the uniform for all the musicians in his big
band – Tito went on talking to the audience at The Palladium.
'If you respect the individuality of each person and bear in mind
the many ingredients needed to make variety, a group of musicians
can create a sound just full of different textures: that's my orchestra.'
Microphone in hand, he turns and sets the rhythm, snapping his
fingers:
'One, two. One, two, three, four.'
The orchestra reacts immediately, and hundreds of pairs of feet
set out to follow that rhythm onto the shining dance floor.
I'll never forget that night all those years ago when Tito Rodríguez
first played '*El que se fue*' (The one who left). It was a brilliant
*pachanga* which lots of us have since used to get our revenge on
people we know:

> *El que se fue no hace falta*
> *hace falta el que vendrá,*
> *en el juego de la vida,*
> *unos vienen y otros van.*
> *Te fuiste por cuenta tuya*
> *buscando ambiente mejor,*
> *hoy estás arrepentido*
> *pués tu puesto se ocupó...*
> *(coro)*
> *A mí no me importas tú*
> *ni diez miles como tú*

*yo sigo siempre en el goce*
*el del ritmo no eras tú.*

The one who left isn't needed
what matters is the one to come
in the game of life
some arrive and others leave.
You left because you chose to
look for something better
now you're sorry you did so
but your place has been taken...
(chorus)
I couldn't care less about you
or ten thousand like you
I still enjoy myself
you're the one left out.

*El que se fue*, version by Tito Rodríguez

I felt like Tito was talking to me when he sang his songs with that soft but penetrating voice of his.

When I arrived in the '*Yores*' from Puerto Rico as a youngster in 1935, Tito was simply one of many badly paid musicians playing in the lowlife bars. The genius he shows in songs like 'The one who left' or '*El Sabio*' (The Wise Man) came from the 1950s, when he was at his height. His reputation may only have been known in our ghetto, but how many of us Latins, in search of the American dream, wished they could be in his shoes? Tito knew he was one of the chosen few, and never forgot what he had been through in the years before he reached the summit.

Puerto Rico is an associated free state in the commonwealth of the United States: in other words, a colony. From the beginning of this century, we inhabitants of that lovely land also known as Borinquen or the Enchanted Isle had been under the influence of Cuban music. We'd also started to rejuvenate our own traditional music known as *La Plena*, a kind of neighbourhood ballad or *bochinche*. These and other Caribbean music forms had to fight against strange rhythms like the One Step or the foxtrot which the colonial power tried to impose. Tunes such as 'Yankee Doodle',

'America', 'Hail Columbia' were core components of the school curriculum.[1]

Despite being the colony of such a powerful country, the economic and social conditions for us Puerto Ricans were not especially appealing, which meant that a great number of us took the first boat or plane we could and headed for the industrial cities of the United States, above all, New York. Out of the frying pan into the fire, as they say, because there we found ourselves in a highly racist society which slotted us into a pecking order alongside the outcast blacks. Dingy apartments in shabby tenements abandoned by the whites in the 1920s now became our homes; they were expensive and unhygienic.[2] I won't even bother to describe my own rathole.

Gradually more people from the Caribbean and later from other Latin American countries found their way here, to join the typical reserve army of the industrial world – the ones who made this nation great by climbing up and down ladders, building, carrying, cooking, washing or hauling anything and everything. This marginal, persecuted minority created 'Spanish Harlem', which we knew simply as 'El Barrio' – a word synonymous with community and warmth, a word to be spoken and written with respect since only those of us who have lived the experience can know what depths of reality and meaning it contains.

> *Qué problema*
> *que no tengo ni un amigo*
> *ni una mujer,*
> *qué problema*
> *que no tengo ni para el cuarto*
> *ni para comer.*

> What a problem
> I haven't got a single friend
> or any woman of my own
> what a problem
> I haven't got money for a room
> or any food at all.

> *Qué problema*, by Noro Morales orchestra, singer
> Vicentio Valdez

As a Puerto Rican, I was one of the first to experience that aggressive social contact which generated a subculture we knew as Niuyorrikan, and then later as Niuyorlatin; the subculture of us third class citizens. It is out of the shit of this marginal slime that the sounds known years later as 'salsa' were born.

I remember those nights when I'd pass my neighbour on his way out into the street in search of some space, some air, carrying his bongo. You knew he was going to set himself up on the street corner, like a million others in the Caribbean or Latin America, to indulge in friendly chat and gossip. You would see him patting the goatskin of his bongo, touching it gently as though caressing it, warming it up before hitting it. Soon we were all with him, us new migrants, with our own percussion instruments, maracas, claves.

And when we'd warmed up a bit we'd beat out the sounds to show our anger, using our instruments to release all the pent-up rage we felt at living on those streets, with just a few dollars in our pockets. We mixed anger, pleasure and weariness, and rediscovered our distant home countries, with their cities and their warm, welcoming, noisy streets. Our music created a sedative for our minds which helped ease the pain of being so far from home and the feeling of being so disregarded in this new country. When it worked, we got what we wanted: everything became one great street party, an unbeatable shared identity in nostalgia.[3]

But I think I'm getting a bit ahead of myself. When I first arrived in New York as a young specialist in dish washing, there were already some Puerto Rican immigrants living in the Barrio who had musical ability. In fact, most of the popular Puerto Rican songs we now know were coined on the streets of New York. These street musicians composed patriotic songs like '*Lamento Borincano*' (Puerto Rican Lament), '*Mi Patria Tiembla*' (My Homeland Trembles), '*Pobre Borinquen*' (Poor Puerto Rico). Once again, they wanted to show their anger, their impotence: they were in the wolf's mouth, but sang against it.

> *Los recibimos con flores,*
> *con música y banderines;*
> *con guitarras y violines,*
> *con frutas y con licores;*
> *contemplamos los colores*
> *de la bandera estrellada,*

*y la isla entusiasmada,*
*jamás ni nunca creyó,*
*verse tan desamparada*
*cuando el Yankee nos copó.*

With flowers we welcomed them
with music and flags;
with guitars and violins,
with fruit and cordials;
we stared at the colours
of their starry banner
and the enthusiastic island
never for once imagined
it would find itself so helpless
when the Yankee took us over.

Cuban or Puerto Rican musicians often came to New York when they were brought over by hotels or cabarets as exotic attractions. Rumour has it that this was how the first Afro-Cuban hit, '*El Manicero*' (The Peanut Vendor) reached the United States in 1930, played by the Cuban Don Azpiazu, leader of the Banda Habana Casino. Apparently, the song was an immediate success, creating a fashion for the rumba overnight. Even today, it is one of the 'anthems' of our identity, still played all over the place in its many different versions.

*Maní,*
*manicero maní.*
*Caserita no te acuestes a dormir*
*sin probar un cucurucho de maní.*
*Cuando la calle sola está,*
*casera de mi corazón,*
*el manicero entona su pregón*
*y si la niña escucha su cantar*
*bajará de su balcón.*

Peanut,
peanut vendor.

Lady don't you go to bed
before you've tried my peanut cone.
When the street is empty
lady of my heart,
the peanut vendor starts his song
and if the young girl hears him
she comes down from her balcony

*El Manicero*, version by Don Azpiazu and the Banda
Habana Casino

## Jazz hits El Barrio

To continue. In the Barrio our neighbours were the black
Americans who practised their music in the yards and streets too,
and formed groups to earn a few cents towards their rent.[4] Living
cheek by jowl like that, we couldn't help picking up the influences
of their jazz music. After all, it came from the same African origins.
Their music was a creature of the night, created in clandestine
drinking dens, dance halls, and the black theatres of New Orleans.[5]
Like all good Latins who like to poke their noses into things, by the
end of the 1930s some of our own musicians were playing in the
new swing jazz bands.

In the early 1940s, I was witness to the bomb that exploded in the
minds of classical jazzmen, who had turned jazz into something
insipid and colourless so as not to offend white ears. The trumpeter
Dizzie Gillespie, the saxophonist Charlie Parker, the pianist
Thelonius Monk burst on the scene with a kind of music called be-
bop, which was rejected as being too violent and radical.[6] Their
crime was to do what they felt like with their instruments to liberate
themselves. As with every liberation struggle, it caused a crisis
amongst a certain kind of audience, but it did offer instrumentalists
and jazz groups the possibility of creating through improvisation.[7]
Latin musicians also benefited from this new freedom.

By 1947 I had clawed my way up to a more lucrative job as a
night-time taxi driver and studied in my spare time. That year
witnessed one of the hottest nights in the history of be-bop. It took
place at a concert in the Pasadena, when the mythical Cuban
drummer and singer Luciano Pozo González, who everyone knew

as 'Chano' Pozo, played the tune '*Manteca*' (Butter) with Dizzy Gillespie. By great good fortune, the concert was recorded, but Pozo's luck ran out only a few hours later when he was murdered in a bar by another Cuban. Pozo's performance that night with Gillespie's band gave a new impetus to the rhythms and percussion of Afro-American jazz.[8]

As you know, our music has always been for dancing. Throughout history, you'll find a constant search for new rhythms to create a new step for dancers.[9] That was why we were bound to get caught up in the swing and be-bop eras in jazz. Everything was for the dancers and our music has always had them in mind.

During the be-bop explosion, Latin musicians managed to fuse rhythmic fire, orchestral colour and jazz expression without ever losing their original Afro-Cuban identity. This was mainly the work of Mario Bauzá and Frank 'Grillo' Machito, who got together to form one of the most important Latin jazz bands ever, not forgetting those which the maestro José Curbelo and the pianist Noro Morales played in. This harmonious fusion which the Latin bands achieved and which proved so popular both with jazz lovers and the followers of Afro-Cuban music did not fall from the sky, nor was it won in a lottery. Mario Bauzá, for example, met up with jazz bands in Cuba and went on to figure in the most prestigious of them, including those of Chick Webb and Cab Calloway, developing new styles and techniques along the way, and showing that in this world quality cannot be bought at the corner drugstore.

These Latin jazz bands, which many people called Afro-Cuban jazz, kept the traditional line-up of trombones, saxes and trumpets to produce a harsh, brilliant sound; they also had a rhythm section based on the piano and the double-bass. What was different was the percussion, where the American set of drums was replaced by the tumbadora, the bongo and the timbal. Some of these orchestras had a 'front-man' or 'front-lady', a singer who led the musicians, and was backed by a chorus.

I may have given the impression that the Latins mopped up other people's influences while bringing nothing to the New York music scene themselves. In fact, the give and take was on both sides. I've already mentioned Pozo and Bauzá. In addition, by the mid-1940s there were jazzmen with powerful lungs in the Latin groups, and Latin percussionists in the jazz bands. The exchange was mutual.

## Mambo fever

And it didn't stop there either. In the late 1940s, my Panamanian friend Juan-de-Dios held a party to celebrate his son's christening. At some point he stopped the band playing and announced he was going to put on the latest craze in New York. What is it, and who plays it? Everyone wanted to know. It was an unknown rhythm called the mambo, played by the Cuban José Curbelo. I swear it had nothing to do with the drink or the heat of the party, but this mambo was a perfect mixture of rhythms, rhythm against rhythm, with no well-defined tonalities or melodies in any of the instruments. To put it another way, it was a rhythmic anarchy first created by Odilio Urfé. It was Cuba that made this sound possible, and it was a great sound.

> *Quién inventó el mambo*
> *que me sofoca,*
> *quién inventó el mambo*
> *que a las mujeres las vuelve locas.*

> Who invented the mambo?
> it takes my breath away
> who invented the mambo?
> it drives all the women crazy.

> *Locas por el mambo,* by Beny Moré with the Pérez Prado band

Brother, you should have seen that mambo fever. From the very start of the fifties it was all the rage. Not just in New York, but throughout the Caribbean and into the rest of Latin America. In fact its lightning success owed a lot to the Cuban, Dámaso Pérez Prado – otherwise known as 'Carefoca' – who was based in Mexico. Pérez used a Cuban percussion section with blaring trumpets, similar to Stan Kenton's jazz band.

'Carefoca' and his dance were at their best on the cinema screen, where you could see his band playing accompanied by a host of spectacular dancers swaying to the music as only they knew how. These scenes were so hot they got the films banned in some countries for obscenity or devil-worshipping. Obsessed with morality and

42

decorum, the Church and the rich in Latin America condemned the mambo as a 'lowlife' sound. Films which contained mambo dancing were treated like today's X-rated films. How scared they were of any expression of popular culture! As ever, it was thanks to this prohibition that the mambo flourished.

And while we were all trying to earn a living as best we could, Cuban musicians went on producing a seemingly endless supply of rhythms, which were taken up and revised by the Latin jazz bands in New York. This was how the chachacha arrived, a slower version of the mambo. It was danced mainly in garages converted into dance halls by youngsters who did not have enough money to go to the big clubs where the mambo was played. Those who have followed the story say it was Enrique Jorrín and his Orquesta América who brought the first chachacha to New York: a tune called 'Silver Star'. Whether or not this is true, it is undeniable that by the mid-1950s, the chachacha was in its heyday, with '*Cerezo en rosa*' (Cherrytree in flower) by Pérez Prado selling a million copies.

> *Oyeme mamá*
> *qué sabroso está*
> *este nuevo ritmo que se llama*
> *Chachachá.*
> *Unísono se canta,*
> *se dice Chachachá,*
> *con unos pasitos*
> *para aquí, para allá.*

> Listen now momma
> to how good it sounds
> this new rhythm called
> the chachacha.
> Just as you sing it
> you call it chachacha
> a few steps here
> a few steps over there.

> *Oyeme mamá*, version by Machito and his orchestra

## Golden Years

Then what happened in June 1950? What always happens: there was another war, this time in Korea. Lots of us Latins had to go off to the front, even though few had much idea of which western civilisation we were supposed to be defending. This caused some disruption to our musical groups, particularly in Puerto Rico, where the trios and quartets playing the bolero and the bolero-son were in hot competition with their counterparts in Mexico.

This was also a period of important advances in sound technology, which led to an upsurge in record production and the music industry in general allowing a greater number of us to buy musical equipment. In fact, it was in 1953 that I was able to buy this record player I still use to listen to the heavy 78rpm records in my modest collection. All this was due to the postwar economic boom which still left us in the ghetto, but at least gave us the chance to earn a few more dollars than before.[10] It was in the mid-1950s that rhythm and blues was promoted beyond its traditional black public by the new, aggressive record companies, who rebaptised it rock and roll for a new, young, white audience. And since the new sound was interesting, we adapted that as well.

*El mambo*
*hizo furor en New York*
*pero el chachachá lo destronó,*
*ahora un nuevo ritmo apareció*
*y es el inquietante rock and roll.*

The mambo
was all the rage in New York
but the chachacha took its place
now a new rhythm has appeared
it's the disturbing rock and roll.

*Rock and Roll*, by La Sonora Matancera, singer, Celia Cruz

How much I miss those years of the fifties and the early sixties! There was so much music, so much creativity! And don't think that this is simply a reaction to seeing my white hairs in the mirror, or that I'm bitter about life, but when I hear what some of those who call themselves singers of son produce today, I think that the past must have been better. Those days really were the golden age of our Afro-Caribbean music.

In the years that straddled the mid-century, the Latin jazz bands in New York saw themselves as heroic for having established a certain distance from the musical influence of Cuba. But the distance was relative. In that concrete city, in the Barrio, every musician's dream was to equal what was being done in Cuba, to enrich it, to go beyond it if possible. Cuba was where everything began and where everything finished; it was the Pole star.

By the late 1940s, the New York Latin bands had managed to secure places of their own in which to create their own music. 'Take us to Broadway and 53rd Street, to the Palladium,' my cab passengers started saying when a number of clubs devoted exclusively to Afro-Caribbean music began to spring up. These clubs gave the groups' creativity free rein, and allowed them to feel they were stars without the pressure of North American promoters. In the past, even the great Latin musicians had been used as 'fillers' in their shows.

At the heart of this club scene was the Palladium. It was a huge dance-hall with capacity for a thousand couples, rescued from closure after the foxtrot lovers had vanished. The Latin bands played our music: what more could we ask? We were better off than in our own countries, with this sophisticated music that brought us the best in jazz and Cuban percussion. Of course, it was all for dancing to. It was frenetic, exciting.[11]

For someone like me who could only go dancing on weekends, the rest of the week was an endless trial. On Saturday I would starch the collar of my shirt, have a good shower, slap on deodorant, perfume and shine my shoes: the Palladium was waiting for me. I was a regular, in the first row of the crowd with my mulatta girlfriend, to get the best view of those magicians and their blissful music.


## Tito Puente

That brings me onto the subject of Tito Puente. I saw him several times playing his incredible music with those drumsticks, sweating like a slave. Tito's rise to fame went something like this. One day, in the late 1940s, Machito was told he would be accompanied by a band of nine musicians known as The Picadilly Boys. This band was led by a young man born in the Barrio who had been lucky enough to study at the Julliard School of Music. At the age of 16 he was playing with the legendary pianist Noro Morales and at 17 had accompanied Machito himself.

He was, of course, Tito Puente, and from that night onwards, he became known as the 'king of the timbal'. Tito made the timbal an integral component of these bands, playing it as though it were his favourite toy. He also introduced a new kind of instrumentation to Afro-Cuban music: the vibraphone played with drumsticks. Soon after he made his debut at the Palladium, Tito disbanded the Picadilly Boys and formed a fabulous orchestra which rivalled those of Machito and his namesake Tito Rodríguez. This orchestra rose to new professional heights, working closely with Stan Kenton, Cal Tjader and Woody Herman.

## Plena y Bomba

One day I was leaning against a wall on the street corner, having a drink and trying to sort out my neighbour's life as usual, when I heard a Puerto Rican sound I hadn't heard in New York before.

It was a type of *plena y bomba*, typical Puerto Rican music, full of picaresque stories, gossip, events from the local neighbourhood or the beach, and the band playing it was the Combo led by Rafael Cortijo, with Ismael Rivera as lead singer. The Combo appeared on the scene in 1955, and the very next year I was in a front row seat for their show at the Teatro Puerto Rico in New York. When they hit the Palladium, the vibrations from their music made the chandeliers swing. One night, the fire department arrived to ask them to calm things down a bit for security reasons; the manager went up onstage and said: 'Hey, Cortijo, no more pachanga, please!'[12]

Their success in Puerto Rico was guaranteed by television, which had just taken off there. They are still among my favourites for their charisma and showmanship, always managing to dance and play their instruments simultaneously. They were poor blacks who never used sheet music when they played, or followed the conventions of ballroom orchestras.[13]

'I spoke of hunger because the group had an anger', Ismael Rivera once said, 'a strength, a rage that came from the poor neighbourhoods, which it expressed unconsciously... do you get me? Those were the days when the blacks in Puerto Rico were rebelling... the first time that blacks got into university... then pow! Cortijo and his Combo appeared, interpreting that hunger, the new movement... it wasn't something planned, it all came from the people, from the blacks... the fact is, people were hungry...' [14]

*Qué le pasó*
*a la mama Inés,*
*qué le pasó,*
*bailó mi bomba y yo no sé qué le pasó.*

*Mi bomba tiene un currulleo curruyú,*
*la tradición de un ritmo viejo que pasó*
*y la forma de bailar la impongo yo.*

*Ella llegó muy tempranito al salón*
*pidió una bomba pa' bailar en un rincón*
*pero parece que la bomba hizo explosión.*

What has happened
to momma Ines,
what's happened to her,
she danced my bomba, and I don't know what's got into her.

My bomba has a currulleo curruyu
the tradition of an old rhythm from the past,
and a way of dancing I invented.

She got to the dancehall early
and asked for a bomba to dance in the corner
but it looks like the bomba exploded.

*Qué le pasó,* version by Rafael Cortijo and Ismael Rivera

When he first heard Ismael Rivera sing, the legendary Beny Moré called him '*El Sonero Mayor*' – son singer supreme – and everyone agreed. '*Maelo*', as Rivera was nicknamed, and Cortijo were men who led turbulent lives, men who came from low down in the social scale, climbed way up high, and fell into all the traps that life sets for people of their sort. But 'grandad Maelo', with his classic shout of '*ecuajey*' in the middle of his songs, or the '*juega*' when he made way for the trumpets, was in the great continuum of black singers like Arsenio Rodríguez, Beny Moré, Tito Rodríguez, Miguelito Valdez.

\* \* \*

While Cortijo and Maelo were on the crest of a wave with their plena y bomba, Cuba was still a decadent tourist's playground under the tutelage of the corrupt dictator, Batista. The image of Cuba created by the United States of the white tourist lolling under a palm tree enjoying his rum and probably the mulatta waitress serving it to him, was still prevalent throughout the continent. Cuba was a tourist's paradise.

But on New Year's Day, 1959, as Fidel Castro's guerrilla army advanced on Havana, Batista fled to the Dominican Republic and Castro set up the first political system in the Americas that was independent of the United States. Nobody imagined then what repercussions this event would generate; some even shrugged it off as a manifestation of Cuba's tropical heritage, but no, the change was real. And Afro-Cuban or Afro-Caribbean music, such an important part of the shared experience and feelings of the Caribbean and Latin American community, changed too. Nothing would be the same again.

> *De mi Cuba*
> *es el mambo, danzonete y el danzón*
> *la guaracha juguetona*
> *te deleita el corazón,*
> *es mi rumba muy caliente*
> *con el mambo y su compás*
> *que recorre el mundo sin cesar.*
> *El bolero es sublime*
> *contagioso y coquetón,*
> *y el afro con mi conga*
> *luce siempre coquetón,*
> *la habanera que es reliquia,*
> *la guajira de verdad,*
> *y hoy en día llegó el chachachá.*

48

This Cuba of mine
produced the mambo, the danzonete and the danzón
the playful guaracha
to delight your heart,
the hot rumba
and the mambo, whose beat
travels endlessly round the world.
The bolero is sublime
infectious and seductive
the Afro in my conga
is always seductive too
the habanera is ancient
really the guajira
and now we have the chachacha.

*Criolla y danza*, version by La Sonora Matancera

# 4

# BRONX REBELS

## From Pachanga to Boogaloo

*New York, paisaje de acero*
*no sé si te odio, no sé si te quiero*
*cuando estoy contigo*
*me siento inquieto por largarme*
*cuando estoy lejos, loco por mirarte;*
*Nueva York, selva de concreto*
*mi corazón guarda el secreto;*
*en tus labios latinos*
*yo vi por primera vez*
*las tradiciones de mis abuelos;*
*mágica ciudadela de sueños dorados*
*capital de desilusiones*
*no sé cómo ni por qué me lleva embrujado*
*donde quiera me recuerdo de New York...*

New York, landscape of steel
I don't know if I hate you or love you
When I'm with you
I'm impatient to get away
When I'm far from you, I'm crazy to see you;
New York, concrete jungle
your secret's buried in my heart:
it was on your Latin lips
I met for the first time
the traditions of my old folk;
magic citadel of golden dreams
capital of disillusion,
I don't know how or why you bewitch me
wherever I go I remember New York...

*Turbulencias latinas*, version by Willie Colón

The 1960s. Who can forget them? In Latin America, Europe, Africa and Asia. Unforgettable. Those were years when everything happened in every sense. What a decade! Our music was not going to stay quiet, letting the world go by. Impossible. Not only did it have to face up to harsh realities, but it had to face up to itself. By the end of the decade it had given us that sound we now hear everywhere: what is now known as salsa was born during those years of struggle in the 1960s.

The arrival in Cuba of a government independent of the United States, and the subsequent complete blockade of that revolution, brought with it a series of repercussions which naturally affected the musical life of the Caribbean and the continent as a whole. The musicians working in the Caribbean tradition in New York, Puerto Rico, Mexico, the Dominican Republic and other countries were left as orphans, since most of their inspiration had come from Cuba. All the rhythms were created there. The great metropolis of New York added flavour and colour thanks to the permanent contact it offered with jazz and other kinds of music from all round the world. But Cuba was the research laboratory. From now on, the musicians had to learn without that school behind them.

Of course, the revolution prompted some of the great Cuban musicians to come to New York, where they were incorporated into the big bands. They were part of a new wave of Cuban immigrants to the United States who left Cuba because they did not agree with the new kind of government, or because of the dreadful stories that the North American press began to fabricate, or simply because they wanted to.

In the United States they did not find paradise. The situation was getting more and more difficult, and they had to share the same conditions of exploitation and marginality as the other rejected minorities. They became part of those who were fighting every day to fend off cultural assimilation, battling not to forget or be ashamed of their own culture. To be allowed to play an honourable part in the existence of their new land. In New York their first port of call was the *Barrio*, that ghetto riddled with unemployment, alcoholism, criminality, drug addiction.

The shock was a brutal one. New York was nothing like Cuba, nor was it anything like the image that had been presented in the movies: it was a sordid, filthy city, with weird people and a totally decadent society.[1] But that was the reality the new Cubans had to share with all the other Latins who had been living in those streets for years; either they faced up to it or did not survive the winter. And that was how their music became not only important but essential, a way of surviving. All they had in their favour in this struggle was their pride and their Barrio, plus a great desire to get out of this circle of human misery. But their sense of disorientation left them exposed and susceptible to other influences outside those of their own music.

## Beatlemania

In October 1962, rock and roll and the twist (which was like drying your back with a towel in both hands, but without the towel) were all the rage, and in England a new song, 'Love Me Do' was launched onto the market by a group called The Beatles. Taking their inspiration from black rock music of the 1950s and riding on an unprecedented publicity campaign, these Liverpudlians succeeded in creating a unique phenomenon in music history: Beatlemania. It marked the birth of pop music, that social movement which was to unify a rebellious new generation throughout the sixties.[2]

When the Beatles came to the United States in 1964, they caused a pop explosion. Caribbean music was now for old folk. Granted, there was still a demand for music with an exotic touch, but this demand was satisfied by bossa nova, a kind of samba rhythm from Brazil. Bossa nova offered a flavour of the tropics that could be easily adapted to tame North American tastes. So in the early 1960s, Latin American musicians had to contend with not only the loss of Cuba, but also with the avalanche of pop music and the bossa nova.

## Pachanga

For a while, the Big Bands managed to survive, thanks to the *pachanga*, the latest sound to come out of Cuba. Created by Eduardo Davison, the pachanga was a cross between the charanga and the chachacha. During the reign of the pachanga, Tito Rodríguez was its foremost exponent, becoming more successful than any of the other Caribbean maestros. He was also one of the first to realise that everything was coming to an end. When he looked around him and saw there was no room anymore for the ostentation and luxury of the Big Bands, Tito Rodríguez opted for a smaller group, and concentrated on playing the bolero, his great native talent. This romantic Tito touched the hearts of social classes far from the Barrio, proving that they felt the same in New York as in the Caribbean.

*Ya llegó, ya llegó*
*el rítmo nacional*
*que siguió al chachachá*
*y le llaman pachanga.*
*Negrita gózalo ahora*
*que pronto llega otro ritmo*
*y quién sabe si este ritmo durará.*

It's here, it's here
our national rhythm
the one following the chachacha
known as the pachanga.
Come on girl enjoy it now
before another rhythm arrives
and replaces this one too.

*Llegó la pachanga*, version by Joe Quijano

## 1963-65: In the Doldrums

To this day, every self-respecting rumba has to have its pachanga. Nevertheless, its decline was inevitable for two reasons. The first was that this cheerful, well-constructed music had less and less to do with the reality of the Barrio. The second was that the sale of alcoholic drink was prohibited in the clubs. Venues such as the Palladium, which had once been centres for the demonstration of all that was best in the Caribbean tradition, fell on hard times and were even forced to close by the mid-1960s. The Big Bands – machines for producing a clean, perfect kind of sound – were in crisis.

As the large clubs closed and the Big Bands faltered, Caribbean music retreated to small venues, to rumbas on street corners or empty lots. For a time the pachanga groups took advantage of this situation, as their sound did not need a big space. But fate was not on their side. The pachanga groups – fronted by José Fajardo, Joe Quijano, Joe Pastrana, Pupy Legarreta, Duboney, Johnny Pacheco and many more – were simply trying to keep alive a sound which, however good to dance to, no longer represented the experience of the Latin community. The pachanga and other sounds of yesterday did not meet the needs of the Barrio's new audiences.

In these years, Caribbean music, whether from pre-revolutionary Cuba, New York, or Puerto Rico, found refuge in the men-only lowlife bars which exist throughout the continent. That was where 'Caribbean music' found its protectors to preserve, enjoy and enrich it, without caring in the least what was said about it. Everywhere else, the North American passion for pop music triumphed.

We are talking about the years 1963-1965. Machito survived these years by continuing to play jazz and attracting a broad jazz audience, which included the Jewish community. Tito Puente also depended on Latin jazz for his survival, while trying to keep pace with the times by including songs from the latest music craze. This approach automatically distanced Machito and Tito from a Latin public that was looking for new emotions and sounds. Rafael Cortijo's Combo, the only new sound created outside Cuba, continued to offer exciting Puerto Rican plenas y bombas. But by the mid-1960s, even his group had suffered blows which almost led to its disappearance: in 1962 the group split, and those who left formed the Gran Combo; shortly afterwards their outstanding singer, Ismael Rivera, was sent to prison for possession of drugs.

## Beats from the Bronx

1966, however, was a year of regeneration when new sounds and ideas began to appear. This was a moment of turbulent social and political upheaval in the United States, Latin America, and the rest of the world. There was the internal debate over the failed Bay of Pigs invasion of Cuba; the Cold War against the countries of the Eastern Bloc, which brought with it the wasting of millions upon millions of dollars on arms in an effort to control the world and outer space as well; the process of decolonisation in Africa; the proliferation of Marxist guerrilla movements in Latin American countries. In many of those countries, the migration to towns and cities accelerated, as did the migration to the United States. Inside the United States itself, this period saw the rise of the civil rights protests, led by the black community, but joined by other marginalised racial minorities, all of them claiming the right to equality.

Few Latin musicians actively engaged in either the civil rights movement or their own communities' struggles. Nevertheless, the new type of music they began to play did give a sense of identity to all those condemned as 'gangsters': workers, shop assistants, illegal migrants, delinquents. Now the bands were creating for the Barrio and no-one else, for its street corners, its misery. This new music did not sound as perfect or as elegant as that played at the Palladium, nor was it: it was the creation of young, inexpert musicians, most of them born in the Bronx, who were trying to establish a cultural identity of their own. They spoke 'Spanglish', that mixture of poor Spanish and worse English.[3]

> *Mete la mano en el bolsillo*
> *saca y abre tu cuchillo*
> *y ten cuidado. Póngame oído*
> *en este barrio muchos guapos han mata'o.*
>
> *Oiga señor*
> *si usted quiere su vida*
> *evitar es mejor*
> *o la tiene perdida*
>
> *Mire señora*
> *agarre bien su cartera*
> *no conoce este barrio*
> *aquí asaltan a cualquiera.*
>
> *En los barrios de guapos*
> *no se vive tranquilo*
> *mide bien tus palabras*
> *o no vales ni un kilo.*

*Beny Moré*
*(author's photo)*

*Orquesta Anacaona. One of several all-female groups popular in Cuba in
the 1940s.*                                    *(author's photo)*

*Rumba dancing in Havana*     *( Rolando Pujol, South American Pictures )*

*Band playing in the 'Bodegüita del Medio', Havana*     *(author's photo)*

*Celia Cruz* *(David Redfern)*

*Ray Barreto and son* *(Leon Morris/Redferns)*

*Memorial to Ismael Rivera*                    *(author's photo)*

*Tito Puente*
*(author's photo)*

*Willie Colón*                               *(David Redfern)*

*Oscar de León in rehearsal*                   *(author's photo)*

*Joe Arroyo*                    *(author's photo)*

*Ruben Blades*                    *(David Redfern)*

*Orquesta de la Luz, Japanese salsa band* (*author's photo*)

*Eddie Palmieri*
(*David Redfern*)

*Irakere from Cuba*                    *( David Redfern )*

*Celina Gonzalez*              *( Lucy Duran/World Circuit )*

*Camina pa'lante, no mires pa'los la'os...*

Put your hand in your pocket
get out your knife and open it
and be careful. Listen to me:
in this neighbourhood
lots of tough guys have killed

Listen to me
if you value your life
best keep out of trouble
or you're likely to lose it

And listen lady
hold your handbag tight
you don't know this neighbourhood
they'll attack anyone here.

Here where the hard guys live
there's no such thing as a quiet life
watch what you say
or you're not worth a cent.

Walk straight ahead, don't look around...

*Calle luna, calle sol,* version by Willie Colón

These new sounds were adopted by Latins, by certain sectors
among the black North American community and by other migrants
who mixed, added, and took bits of Cuban and black music, rock
music, Caribbean and African folklore, introducing instruments
which had never been part of the Caribbean tradition before. Despite
the obvious recycling, it sounded authentic and exciting.
Unfortunately, those who had been heroes of Caribbean music in
the previous decade decided to reject this new tendency, dismissing
it as a betrayal, a defeat for Latin traditions.

But it was no such thing. On the contrary, it was trying to rescue
tradition, identity, authenticity. Naturally enough it had to breathe
fresh life into the music by updating it and by introducing the new

techniques and ideas that pop music was creating in the world of recording. Okay, so some notes were lengthened artificially in the studio, and new instruments such as electronic keyboards were brought in from soul, jazz and rock music. It was also true that the sounds were no longer as sweet and pure as those produced by the Big Bands in their heyday: everything now was harsh, inexpert, rebellious, dissonant, aggressive, insistent. The purists were horrified at how the image and the sweet tones of the *sonero* had changed. But now the singers' voices reflected the reality of life as it was lived in the big city neighbourhoods. They were closer to their black fathers and grandfathers who'd protested against the banning of the son in Cuba some forty years beforehand than people imagined. Like their forefathers, they shouted their defiance of anything remotely connected to institutions. It was spontaneous, uncalculated, but true to the daily reality of the time. And the new sound spread from the Barrio in New York without any publicity or fanfare, against the prevailing current.

## Boogaloo

*(acompañando a las palmas)*
*uh, ah, uh, ah, uh, ah, uh, ah*

*(coro)*
*ayayai Micaela sé votó*
*que sé votó, que sé votó*
*ayayai Micaela sé votó*

*(solo)*
*Cuando yo baile con ella*
*Micaela se votó,*
*el boogalú lo bailó*
*y yo sé que ella es candela*

*Ayayai Micaela sé votó (coro)*
*y cuando yo baile con ella, atrás me dejó, (solo)*
*ayayai Micaela sé votó (coro)*

*(solo)*
*Micaela cuando baila,*
*el boogalú arrebata*
*toda la gente la llama*
*la reina del boogalú.*

*ayayai Micaela sé votó (coro)*
*que sé votó, que sé votó, que se votó (solo)*
*ayayai Micaela sé votó (coro)*
*y cuando yo bailo con ella, atrás me dejó (solo)*
*ayayai Micaela sé votó (coro)*
*que sé votó, que sé votó, que sé votó (solo).*

(sung while clapping)
uh, ah, uh, ah, uh, ah, uh, ah...

(chorus)
Ay ay ay Micaela is long gone,
long gone, long gone,
ay ay ay Micaela's long gone

(solo)
When I danced with her
Micaela lost her head
the boogaloo sent her
I know she's a hot dancer

ay ay ay Micaela's long gone (chorus)
when I dance with her
she leaves me way behind
ay ay ay Micaela's long gone (chorus)

(solo)
when Micaela dances
the boogaloo is a sensation
everyone knows
she's the queen of boogaloo.

ay ay ay Micaela's long gone (chorus)

long gone, long gone, long gone (solo)
ay ay ay Micaela's long gone (chorus)
when I dance with her
she leaves me way behind (solo)
ay ay ay Micaela's long gone (chorus)
long gone, long gone, long gone (solo)

*Micaela*, version by Pete Rodríguez

The boogaloo, or *bugalú* as it is written in Spanish, was perhaps the first Caribbean rhythm to be invented in New York itself. 'Micaela' by the pianist Pete Rodríguez was the start of a dance fever that took over from the pachanga. The boogaloo was an uncomplicated rhythm, with simple words, constantly interrupted by shouts and applause. It was something almost done out of despair, a defiant shout proclaiming that it belonged exclusively to one particular corner of New York City.[4] In purely musical terms it was of doubtful value because it was produced by kids off the streets, used to messing around. But whatever it may have lacked in quality, it made up for in authenticity: it was very much their thing, our thing, as was shown by its immediate popularity.

Its words hopped from Spanish to English. It was probably influenced too much by pop music, perhaps with an eye to gaining access to the North American market. The switching between two languages was another symptom of the transculturisation that was taking place. Some say it began as a 'soul' version of the Cuban guajira; others maintain it was a way of intepreting the Cuban guajira via Puerto Rican New York; most people say it was a mixture of pop music and the Cuban son (which has always been so accommodating, so open to influences, so ready to adapt itself to any new sound).

Although the boogaloo was a short-lived craze, all the Latin bands played it. José Calderón, nicknamed Joe Cuba, was the boogaloo singer most idolised by the Latin community. Joe championed the use of both Spanish *and* English in his songs, which themselves made constant references to life in the Barrio. His modest sextet consisting of a singer, timbal, tumbadora, piano, double bass and vibraphone (an instrument used in Latin jazz but virtually unknown in Caribbean music) epitomised the changes in our musical world, so soon after the boom of the Big Bands.

*Así se goza (coro)*
*y es que la rumba es sabrosa (solo)*
*así se goza,*
*baila, baila, baila la rosa*
*así se goza,*
*mira si es que te pica la mano, andá.*

*así se goza,*
*así se goza,*
I'll never go back to Georgia
I'll never go back...


That's the way (chorus)
because the rumba is exciting
that's the way,
dance, dance, the rose is dancing
that's the way,
and if it pricks your hand, too bad.

that's the way,
that's the way
I'll never go back to Georgia
I'll never go back...

*El Pito*, version by Joe Cuba and his sextet

# 5

# FANIA ALLSTARS

## and 'Our Latin Thing'

*Para ser rumbero tú tienes que haber llorado;*
*para ser rumbero tú tienes que haber reído,*
*tú tienes que haber soñado, haber vivido;*
*para ser rumbero tú tienes que sentir por dentro*
*emociones dulces que agiten tus sentimientos,*
*si no naciste con clave entonces no eres rumbero;*
*podrás cantar con sentido, podrás tener buena voz*
*pero ser rumbero nunca si te falta corazón;*
*para ser rumbero tienes que amar a la gente*
*y tener el alma tan clara como el sol de oriente*
*tú tienes que ser sincero y entonces serás rumbero...*
*El rumbero es ser humano con su risa y su dolor*
*expresando sentimientos con el golpe del tambor,*
*debe ser sincero para tocar la rumba, ay Dios!*

To play the rumba you need to have cried;
to play the rumba you need to have laughed,
you need to have dreamt, to have lived;
to play the rumba you need to feel inside
sweet emotions that awaken your feelings,
if you weren't born with feeling you can't be a rumba player;
you can sing with feeling, you can have a good voice
but never be a rumba player if you have no heart;
to play the rumba you need to love people
and to have a soul as clear as the sun in the east
you need to be sincere, and then you'll be a rumba player...
the rumba player is a human being with his laughter and his grief
expressing his feelings to the beat of the drum,
above all, you have to be sincere to play the rumba!

*'Para ser rumbero'*, version by Roberto Roena

63

Hello, hello, okay: everybody happy?
yeah!!
Everybody hot?
yeah!!
So now take off my clothes!!
Okay we need a bottle we got bottle
Right we wanna welcome and compliment, okay
Okay *que pare* Chango.

Right now I want to introduce a man who made a real hit right here in New York, in Brooklyn...Ladies and gentlemen, please welcome...direct from Puerto Rico....uuuuuuuggggg... Bobby Cruz and Ricardo Ray on piano, gimme eeeeeyyyyy!!!

While we're waiting expectantly for the orchestra to begin, we cajole them into starting with our clapping and chanting:

plaplapla
    plaplá
        plaplapla
            plaplá

                plaplapla
                  plaplá

Can't you hear the clave, what's going on?
Cheo Feliciano gives the signal. And Ricardo sets his ten magic fingers twinkling on the keys, letting loose those volleys of sound that strike into the deepest part of our beings. Our hair stands on end, hot and cold shivers run up and down our spines. The entire orchestra strikes up. The trumpets pierce our ears with indescribable pleasure, we want to embrace the whole world. We jump for joy, whistle, dance. Why are you crying? I've no idea, and couldn't care less. Listen, here comes the voice of Bobby!!

*Yo vine pa'veriguar*
*lo que aquí está sucediendo,*
*que hace tiempo que no vengo*
*y no me quieren contar.*

I came to find out
what's going on here
I haven't been for some time
and nobody wants to tell me

And we all shouted the chorus at the top of our lungs:

Now I'm here!
    now I'm here!
        now I'm here!
            now I'm here!
*Ahora vengo yo*, Fania Allstars

Then we forget everything. Why wait to go to heaven or hell if
the beat of the drums is offering us such celestial devilry? My God,
listen to those sounds and forgive me for being an atheist, but I have
no doubts about humanity!!

The film, '*Nuestra Cosa Latina*', ('Our Latin Thing'), made us
feel good to be alive and proud to be Latin with hot, dancing blood
in our veins. It focused on a concert the Fania Allstars had given on
21 August 1971 in the seedy, old Cheetah club near the Bronx. Apart
from the music, the film brought home to us a good few things. For
the first time, it showed Latin Americans outside the United States
the reality for the '*Yores*' in the Big Apple. There was the famous
Barrio and its ancient, filthy tenements, with human flesh crammed
into every inch, their patched clothing hanging out to dry in the
windows. The film even showed the clandestine cockfights and the
santería ceremonies. In short, it showed us all the wretchedness and
isolation people had refused to believe could exist in the 'capital of
the world'. 'Our Latin Thing' was the first documentary on the
origins of our music as an expression of Latin American social
identity.

When Latins in South America saw the film, they were amazed at
what their counterparts in New York had done. Up until then,
knowledge of Caribbean dance music in the countries south of
Venezuela and Colombia had been limited to the chachacha, the
mambo, the bolero and the occasional jolly guaracha in old Mexican
and Cuban films. 'Our Latin Thing' offered a whole new dimension
to this music.

That night in the Cheetah Club the Fania musicians gave it all they had. We could not take our eyes off Ray Barreto on the tumbadora, or Roberto Roena on the bongos; Orestes Vilató on the timbales; '*El Malo*' Willie Colón, Barry Rogers and Reinaldo Jorge on the trombones; or Héctor '*Bomberito*' Zarzuela and Larry Spencer on trumpet; or on the piano, the 'wonderful Jew', Larry Harlow (although Ricardo Ray stood in for him whenever Bobby Cruz sang); Bobby Valentín on the electric bass, and '*El Gordo*' Yomo Toro playing his heart out on the cuatro. What more could you ask?

*Somos las Estrellas Fania*
*gente de todas las razas,*
*comemos de un mismo plato*
*y usamos la misma taza.*

*Nos llevamos como hermanos*
*sin rencor, con alegrías,*
*aquí no existen envidias*
*todos nos damos la mano.*

*Por eso cuando cantamos*
*lo hacemos de corazón,*
*y alegramos corazones*
*con nuestra salsa y sabor,*
*somos los embajadores*
*de la paz y del amor.*

*Somos las estrellas Fania*
*que a toditos saludamos,*
*venga un abrazo sincero,*
*venga un abrazo de hermano...*

We are the Fania Allstars
people from every race
we eat from the same plate
and drink from the same cup.

We get along like brothers
with no resentment, only pleasure,

none of us is jealous
we all give each other a hand.

That's why when we sing
we sing from the heart,
and we gladden other hearts
with our salsa and our flavour
we are the ambassadors
of peace and of love.

We are the Fania Allstars
we say hello to you all
here's our sincere embrace
the embrace of a brother...

*Hermandad Fania*, Fania Allstars

So much for the instrumentalists. As for the vocalists, they were represented by no less than: Héctor Lavoe, Ismael Miranda, Pete 'Conde' Rodríguez, Bobby Cruz, Adalberto Santiago, Santos Colón and José 'Cheo' Feliciano who, to everyone's delight, had overcome the difficult obstacles in his path and was there full of life. Laughing and leaping around as he directed this constellation of all stars was their co-founder, the flute-playing musical director Johnny Pacheco, 'another of your servants'.

The Fania Allstars gave us mind-blowing songs where instrumentalists and singers were all working together as one. That was the key. A massive demonstration of how an integrated group could sound, even if their aims were commercial. The main objective of the Fania people was to expand, introduce and sell this new sound without sacrificing its two basic ingredients: the musicians' spontaneity and freedom to sing and play whatever their enthusiasm dictated, without forgetting the dancer.[1]

In fact, well before the Cheetah show, an earlier one had taken place in 1968. Its importance had been limited, though, because it had turned into an experimental jazz jam session. Similar Latin jam sessions had been promoted throughout the 1960s in an attempt to discover the anxiously awaited new alternatives for Latin music. Sometimes the young musicians got together without the direct participation of the record companies; at others it was the companies themselves who brought together their musicians and added special guests. These sessions allowed the musicians the freedom to create spontaneously and to demonstrate just what their talents were. Typical of these were the Alegre, Cesta, and Tico Allstars. The public for these sessions was very small, and the results did not find a huge audience because they offered little that was suited to the dance floor. Anything that cannot be danced to is unlikely to be very popular among the Latin public. Nevertheless, these Allstar sessions were a learning experience.

It was during the Cheetah show in 1971 that we witnessed the emergence of a new sound, a sound which owed something to the harmonic and rhythmic patterns of the Cuban son, but which was much more the creation of Latin musicians in New York. It was what they had been searching for throughout the 1960s.

## Birth of Fania Records

The skinny moustache-less man who conducted the Fania bands in the Cheetah club concert was Johnny Pacheco. In 1964, to explore the possibilities of the son, Pacheco had changed the format of his *pachanga* band into a larger, Cuban-style band (two trumpets, a tres, piano, bongo, cowbells, congas) like Sonora Matancera. Pacheco refused to give in to the North American influences which Caribbean musicians had to contend with while they struggled to make a living during those difficult days. But as well as being a good judge of what his Latin public wanted, he also knew it was essential to rescue Caribbean music from the marginal, anonymous position it had fallen into. That was why he got together with the Jewish lawyer Jerry Masucci to form the Fania record company.

As so often where popular culture is concerned, there has been a lot of speculation as to where the name of the company came from. Some people have even said it was Masucci's mother's name; but the truth is that Fania is a Yoruba word from Afro-Cuba and is the title of one of the first Cuban sons that Pacheco adapted for his new line-up. Fania had modest beginnings: Pacheco and Masucci started by plodding from one record shop to another, flogging their records from the trunk of Masucci's car. At that time, the records consisted solely of music by Pacheco's group. Then two years later they signed up the 'marvellous Jew' Larry Harlow, a pianist who had worked in jazz and rock music, but who had one day become addicted to Caribbean rhythms and had formed his own group to play them. At the same time, Fania signed the bassist Bobby Valentín's band. And a few months later they attracted the tumbadora player Ray Barreto, who had a considerable reputation among the Latin community.

In 1967, the Fania company recorded a young trombonist who had to dye his hair grey and wear a false moustache to get into nightclubs to play, because he was only sixteen years old. This was Willie Colón, who in a few short years became one of the foremost inspirations behind everything that was happening in the Caribbean and throughout the continent. But in those days, the established musicians believed Colón's group epitomised all the bad influences of New York. 'Tito Puente, Ray Barreto and others used to make fun of the young groups,' says Colón. 'They were refusing to see the obvious... they said we knew nothing. That we shouldn't bring different styles together, like the Cuban *guaguancó* with North American songs, the Puerto Rican bomba with jazz or anything else. But for those of us who had grown up in the Barrio listening to all these influences, there was no contradiction in bringing them together...all they did really was to try to stand in our way and reject us. They stuck to a concept of Afro-Caribbean music as though it had to be performed like a rite or a Shakespeare play, with nothing changed.'[2]

One day in the Barrio, the young Willie Colón ran into exactly what he needed to put his mould-breaking project into practice and gain immediate recognition: Héctor Lavoe's voice. It had just the right tone of lowlife intrigue to dramatise all the violent events that characterised the neighbourhood they were brought up in. Songs born in the dark corners of that Barrio which still resonate today like '*Todo tiene su final*' (Everything Comes to an End) or '*El día de mi suerte*' (The Day My Luck Changes).

*(coro)*
*Pronto llegará el día de mi suerte*
*sé que antes de mi muerte*
*seguro que mi suerte cambiará*

*Cuando niño mi mamá se murió*
*solito con el viejo me dejó*
*me dijo solo nunca quedarás*

*porque él no esperaba una enfermedad.*
*A los 10 años papá se murió*
*se fue con mamá para el más allá*
*y la gente decía al verme llorar*
*no llores nene que tu suerte cambiará.*
*Y cuándo será?*

*(coro)*

*Esperando mi suerte quedé yo*
*pero mi vida otro rumbo cogió*
*sobreviviendo en una realidad*
*de la cual yo no podía ni escapar.*
*Para comer hay que buscarse el real*
*aunque sea con uno de la sociedad.*
*A la cárcel me escribe una amistad:*
*no te apures que tu suerte cambiará.*
*Oye, verás!*

(chorus)
Soon the day my luck changes will arrive
I know before I die
my luck is bound to change

When as a child my momma died
and left me on my own with poppa
you'll never be alone he said
thinking he'd never get ill.
But when I was ten he died as well,
and joined her in the great beyond,
and seeing how I cried, people said
don't cry kid, your luck is bound to change.
When will that be?

(chorus)

I waited and waited for my luck to change
by my life took another turn
trying to survive in a reality
it was impossible to escape from.
You have to have money to eat

70

even if the money is not yours.
Now a friend of mine writes to me in jail:
don't worry, your luck will change.
You just wait and see!

*El día de mi suerte,* version by Willie Colón

Whatever it lacked in quality, the sound produced by Colón and his singer Hector Lavoe made up for in authenticity and a sense of identity for a public who recognised their own daily lives in it. What more could they ask for? Soon the trombone, played freely and with great musical violence, became the symbol of the new Latin music emerging in New York. Colón and Lavoe brought Caribbean music back to the Barrio – where it really belonged – after the distance that had grown up with the pomp of the big bands. And they were right: this was how salsa was born and grew.

Another valuable contributor to this innovation in New York was Ray Barreto, who began to play during his military service in Germany. Although he often worked in Latin jazz, many of his compositions referred to the Barrio. It was Barreto who succeeded in getting the boogaloo tune 'Watussi 65' into the national US Hit Parade. Soon afterwards, he changed the format of his group, and began to work energetically for the Fania project.

When I was talking earlier of the film 'Our Latin Thing', I mentioned a talented pianist called Ricardo Ray. This 'magic fingers' first appeared in 1965 with an array of new and challenging sounds that immediately classified him as one of the 'hardliners'. Like most of the others, the vocalist Bobby Cruz was a youngster from the Barrio without much experience, but his voice created confidence, energy, friendship. The words of their songs were drawn from the Puerto Rican cultural heritage and the religious cosmovision of Afro-Cuban santería. Far from seeming out of place, this helped the new sound conquer the sultry Caribbean cities. The arrangements allowed each instrument to display their qualities and possibilites all the time, as if they were crying out: 'Take it, it's yours, devour it!' Which we did until we were full to bursting. This lasted from the mid-1960s till the mid-1970s. If you want to know the personal history of any real rumba fanatic, ask them about '*Richies jala jala*', '*Sonido bestial*', '*Aguzate*' or '*El diferente*' and you'll be amazed

how many nightlife experiences they can recall, as they drift back
into their memories.

*Ay qué dilema tan grande*
*este problema que tengo*
*si no llevo la contraria*
*no puedo vivir contento.*

*Hay quien se conforma en ver*
*cómo la vida le pasa*
*sin tratar de corregir,*
*al mundo cambiarle nada.*

*(coro)*
*Más yo buscaré la forma*
*de ser siempre diferente*
*para que no diga la gente*

*(solo)*
*que Ricardo lo copió ...*

What a dilemma I've got
with this problem of mine
if I can't contradict
I can never be happy.

Some people just like to see
life passing them by
without trying to change it
taking the world for what it is.

(chorus)
But I'll find a way
always to be different
so that no one can say

(solo)
Ricardo only copied things

*El Diferente*, version by Ricardo Ray

By the early 1970s, the seven groups on the Fania label were working mostly within the tradition of the Cuban son. Their arrangements were clear and attractive, reflecting something of their urban, cosmopolitan surroundings. By now there was a typical New York line-up and sound to these bands. The percussion section was Cuban, with tumbadora, timbal and bongo. The brass section was more New York: a combination of trumpets as with the son groups, and trombones, which were soon to be one of the identifying characteristics of what came to be called salsa. There was almost always a piano as well, and sometimes a double bass, a tres, maracas, clave, and the *güiro* – the last three of these usually played by the singer and/or the chorus. So it was that from the marginal area of the Barrio, with the blessing of the son and the fusion of influences drawn from a multitude of traditions, a sound that was specifically our own was born.

*Nací moreno*
*porque así tenía que ser*
*por mi color*
*soy muy fácil de entender.*

*Cantando voy*
*haciendo el mundo feliz*
*pues soy candela, palo y piedra*
*hasta morir.*

*Nací moreno*
*porque así tenía que ser*
*y en mi cantar*
*yo voy a explicar por qué*

*Yo nací*
*y mi madre fue la rumba*
*y a mi padre*
*lo apodaban guaguancó.*

*Fui bautizado con tres toques de conga*
*en un manatial de sabor,*
*ah, caray!*

*(coro)*
*Moreno soy*
*porque nací de la rumba*
*y el sabor*
*yo lo heredé del guaguancó.*


I was born black
because that's the way it was
thanks to my colour
I am easy to understand.

I go round singing
to make the world happy
because I am flame, stick and stone
until my dying day.

I was born black
because that's the way it was
and in this song of mine
I'm going to tell you why

I was born
and my mother was the rumba
my father was
nicknamed the guagancó.

I was baptised to three conga beats
in a rushing spring of flavour
oh yes, oh yes

(chorus)
I'm black
because I was born of the rumba
and I inherited my flavour
from the guaguancó.

*Moreno soy*, version by Bobby Valentín

# 6

# SALSA IS BORN!

'Before the word salsa was coined, people who knew music used to say: son, guaracha, danzón, chachacha; but those who weren't musical experts found this hard to follow. In Fania we thought we needed a word as simple as 'yes', 'rock and roll' or 'country music', so we hit on 'salsa'... when I made the film 'Salsa' I registered it, and I have the copyright.'
Jerry Masucci, director of Fania Records

It was in the 1970s that the so-called 'salsa' boom took off, and the word, 'salsa' became identified with Latin music throughout the world. It gave rise to a number of questions similar to those asked of jazz and rock, which paradoxically shared its black origins. At its simplest, this involved a discussion of how the term itself was coined. As I explained in my introduction, the word had always been around. But it was the Fania company who knew it would be the word they could use to gain immediate acceptance in the New York Barrio and in the cities of the Caribbean. It was Fania who really promoted the word.

I mentioned earlier that the term was used by Ignacio Piñeiro as early as the 1920s. It surfaced again with the Cuban group, Los Salseros, led by Cheo Marquetti during the 1940s, and both Beny Moré and Celia Cruz used to shout it in the middle of their songs before making way for the instrumental solos. The usage closest in time to the salsa boom can be found in 1966 when the Venezuelan presenter Danilo Phidias Escalona used it on his radio programme '*La hora del sabor, la salsa y el bembé*' (Hour of Caribbean flavour, sauce and lips), in which he played pachangas, rumbas, guaguancós, boleros, chachachas and mambos: in other words, just about every Caribbean rhythm. At around the same time, also in Venezuela, an LP by Federico and his Combo Latino came out, entitled '*Llegó la salsa*' (Salsa Has Arrived). In New York, it seems to have been used first by Ray Barreto, when he called one of his compositions *'Salsa y dulzura'* back in the 1960s. The Hermanos Lebrons also had a tune called *'Salsa y control'*. But nobody had used it in a more general sense.

In the 1970s, Larry Harlow came close when he recorded for Fania one of his best albums, called simply *'Salsa'*. This record is also important for dedicating two tracks to the charanga, a rhythm that had become eclipsed due to the popularity of the pachanga. Harlow had been in Venezuela where, according to the violinist Alfredo de la Fé, he had run into a guy who was always shouting *'salsa! salsa! salsa!'* in his concerts. Seeing how enthusiastically the public reacted to this, Jerry Masucci and Izzy Sanabria noted it down as one of the ideas they should explore for their expanded musical company.[1] This is proof that while the Venezuelans did not invent the term, they did a lot to raise its profile.

But what exactly is salsa? What does it represent musically? This is the second and perhaps more serious point of debate about it. The Cubans, for example, say it is simply a modern version of the son, and never tire of repeating how many musicians and record companies took advantage of the US blockade against their country to plagiarise their music in a scandalous way. Some Cuban exiles agree. Some Cuban musicians even took out lawsuits after they discovered their own compositions had been claimed by other groups, or simply published with the letters 'D.R.' (*Derechos Reservados* – Rights Reserved) which are meaningless apart from concealing who the original artist was.

To some extent the Cubans are right to be upset. But just as it is impossible to say that salsa is a genuinely authentic creation of the New York Latins, so it would be false to see it as simply an updated version of Cuban music. The complex social situation in the New York Barrio was unlike anything experienced in post-revolutionary Cuba and meant that the music produced there had very different connotations from earlier forms. Salsa also depended on the co-existence of people from different countries with varied experiences which gave it new possibilities. The Afro-Cuban roots it sprang from were given fresh arrangements, thanks to technological developments and the aggressive style of a new generation.

Many outside the salsa camp constantly point to its lack of a well-defined identity. What these detractors refuse to understand is that salsa has never defined itself as a specific musical genre, but rather as a broadly based libertarian and pluralist sound, able to accommodate all the emotions generated by its surroundings. That is how it grew. As it was such a special conglomeration, it took in a whole series of rhythms, sounds and tendencies which are still present in the cities of the Caribbean. To most listeners a pachanga, a son, a rumba, plena or a guaguancó are all salsa; the chachacha, the guajira, the mambo, the bomba, the bolero and the boogaloo are all salsa too. Sometimes even the Venezuelan gaita, the merengue from the Dominican Republic, and the Colombian cumbia are slung into the same basket.

Since it is such an amalgam of styles and such a free, unregimented kind of music, salsa is able to go wherever it wishes, paying tribute to all the gods but submitting to none, since its ultimate objective is always dancing, a profane, wild enjoyment. So salsa has something for every age and taste: salsa specifically for dancing (although all its versions can be danced to); salsa that tells stories, gossip, picaresque tales; salsa that is romantic, sentimental, intimate, erotic; salsa that is rebellious, nonconformist, against authority, and nationalist; experimental salsa; religious, mystic salsa based on santería.

Because it can unite all these qualities, and because of the emotions it can arouse, salsa helps give a sense of identity to the poor inhabitants of Panama City or Portobelo in Panama; Caracas or Maracaibo in Venezuela; Guayaquil in Ecuador; Santo Domingo in the Dominican Republic. It is enjoyed and worshipped in Cali or Barranquilla in Colombia; San Juan, Santurce or Ponce in Puerto Rico; Lima in Peru; in Miami or East Harlem in New York. And those who describe themselves as salsa followers are not limited to the cities. There are said to be about sixty million people who at the slightest sign of a salsa party find their 'black globules' dancing about inside them, to use a typically Cuban expression.

Given all this, who can deny that salsa is a spontaneous political phenomenon springing from an economically underprivileged social sector? Not only did salsa succeed in breaking down ideological barriers through gaining acceptance on both left and right, but it broke through the continent's territorial barriers as well, becoming an important vehicle for integration and identity. And in Europe, isn't salsa synonymous with all that it means to be Latin?

Of course there were some who attacked salsa when they found out it had first emerged in New York. In certain sectors it was seen as yet another 'opiate' invented by the gringos to control and neutralise popular consciousness. It would have been terrific if it had seen the light of day in Havana, San Juan, Cali, or Caracas, but just as this new music came to be called salsa and not something else, so it happened to be born in the city of skyscrapers. That's all there was to it. New York offered a variety of indispensable factors that no other city in the Caribbean had.

First and foremost there was the existence of an army of un-and under-employed trying to find a place in a society that continually rejected them. They were a marginalised and brutalised sector of society which saw in this new music a way to cling on to their identity, especially Puerto Ricans who did not want to be seen as Yankees even if this was not translated into a massive political demand for independence. Salsa was born like a desperate cry in the night, a cry which proclaimed the value of all that was mulatto, Caribbean, Latin, and Indian in its musicians. Salsa was the result of this fight against the aggressive cultural assimilation they were continually submitted to.

On the other hand, there is no doubt that the term salsa was misused out of commercial greed until it became more important than the music itself. But it is still there and I am sure it will survive. Like the tango, the ranchera, reggae or the son itself, it is truly popular music, and whatever comes from the people, lives in the people and draws its life from them.

> *La salsa que me gusta a mí*
> *es sin tomate y sin ají*
> *sin condimento ni sazón*
> *no se cocina en el fogón*
> *óyelo bien.*

> *(coro)*
> *Que me den de tu salsa, compay*
> *que me den de tu salsa.*

> *La salsa que te traigo yo*
> *es salsa con ritmo de son*
> *condimentado con bongó*
> *y con sabor a guaguancó*
> *óyelo bien*

*(coro)*
*Compay salsa soy yo*
*compay salsa.*

*Salsa que no tiene*
*tomate, ají ni limón,*
*salsa con maracas, güiro y bongó*
*esta salsa la baila Tata y Ramón.*

The salsa that I like
has no tomato or chilli pepper
no condiment or seasoning
and – listen to me now – is not cooked in any fire.

(chorus)
Give me your salsa friend,
give me your salsa.

The salsa that I'm offering you
is salsa with the rhythm of son
spiced with bongo
and the flavour of guaguancó
listen to me now

(chorus)
I'm your friend the salsa
friend salsa am I

Salsa that has no
tomato, pepper or lemon,
salsa with maracas, güiro and bongo
salsa danced by Tata and Ramón

*Compay salsa*, version by Vitín Avilés

By 1973, the records and the film made by the Fania Allstars at
the Cheetah club were well-known across Latin America. Fania had
succeeded, not so much with a film, but more with a social document

– the joyful expression of a harsh reality. Gradually they began to achieve their most desired objective: to break down the social and generational barriers surrounding Caribbean music. It was no longer 'scandalous music for blacks, the poor, bums and drunks'. Nor was it simply music for middle-aged men in seedy bars and brothels.

## 'Salsa': the Film

Given the success of the first film, Fania decided to set up another concert to provide the focus for a second film. The cameraman León Gast, who directed 'Our Latin Thing', intended to use the same structure, alternating scenes from the concert with others from the daily life of the Hispanic community in New York. At the suggestion of other Latins who worked in US television, but knew little about Afro-Caribbean music, it was decided to add clips from old Hollywood films, in which famous Latin artists appeared. In order to reach a wider public, the African saxophonist Manu Dibango, who at that time was very popular thanks to his 'Soul Makossa', and the American drummer Bill Cobham, were not only invited to play alongside the Allstars, but were given their own solo spots. So ambitious had Fania now become that they hired the Yankee stadium for the concert, and it was here on the night of 24 August 1973 that almost 50,000 people came to take part in the first mass homage to Caribbean music, the genuine expression of Latin identity.

The concert began with the Típica 73 group, recently formed from musicians who had split from Ray Barreto. After them came Mongo Santamaría, a giant of Latin jazz. The third group was the Gran Combo from Puerto Rico. Their choreography and excellent vocalist Andy Montañez set the tone for the evening. Emotions were running high; some were getting anxious as they waited for the main attraction. At last, the Fania Allstars filed out onstage one by one, and stood by their instruments. The last to emerge was Johnny Pacheco. The Yankee stadium went wild.

Pacheco gave instructions. Everything was ready. Then he stood in front of the silent, expectant audience, grabbed the mike and started to improvise as the percussion section thundered into action.

*Saludando señores*
*con un ritmo tropical,*

*descarga de bongó*
*ton bom bim con quin ca*
*timbala catira quincalá*
*can ca somá calá quili bimpum*
*que lo invita a guarachar*
*a nuestro hermano*
*y con el pueblo*
*que se encuentra aquí*
*alala alala alalala*
*Vaya!!...Abre!!...Harlow!!!!*

Greetings to you all
with a tropical rhythm
the sound of the bongo
*ton bom bim con quin ca*
*timbala catira quincalá*
*can ca soma cala quili bimpum*
calling you to dance
you there brother
all the people here
alala alala alalala
Over to you...Harlow!!!!

Pacheco shouts, and Larry is off. All the instruments come in together; the choruses add their emotion; Héctor Lavoe gives his soneo free rein, the two giants Barreto and Mongo Santamaría launch into a breathtaking duel on their tumbadoras... and the safety barriers collapse. The audience can't bear it any longer: they want to get close to their idols. But with this, the concert is over almost as soon as it has started, because it is strictly forbidden for the public to spill onto the 'holy of holies' baseball pitch.

In spite of this disappointment, Fania decided to complete the film which they called 'Salsa'[2], combining the footage shot in the Yankee stadium with the clips from Hollywood films. But the work was left in unskilled hands, which meant that the final product contained inaccuracies and gaps, and left a lot to be desired, The Hollywood sequences with Dezy Arnas, Dolores del Río and the Castro Sisters jar with the original intention of the film. The idea, it seems, was to show that Latins could be successful in North

American showbusiness. But the Hollywood clips just looked like space-fillers. Meanwhile, there was no attempt to show the real social roots of salsa.

Despite these faults, the film was well received both in Latin America and further afield. It gave the term 'salsa' a great deal of exposure, not to mention Fania itself. Many more people saw it than the earlier 'Our Latin Thing' so it achieved its desired result. Whereas the first film had been intended to spread the Latin musical message beyond the ghetto and the Caribbean, 'Salsa' was made in order to blast the sounds to the farthest corners of the earth. While 'Our Latin Thing' remained the real expression of Latin music, 'Salsa' was the film with the greater export potential.

## The Fania music machine

By now, Fania had created a structure which enabled it to expand and actively seek new markets. The challenge was enormous, as the recording and pressing of discs was only the start. The most difficult task was to take on the big multinational companies who controlled the media and knew how to pull the publicity strings. But the spirit of fellowship and co-operation within Fania was so strong that they managed to overcome all these problems. They relied on Jerry Masucci's business acumen, on the lack of interest shown by the US multinationals who were obsessed by rock, and above all on the popularity – bordering on idolatry – which their musicians enjoyed. Johnny Pacheco had always been a sound judge of public tastes.

It is worth mentioning here the opportunities Fania offered its musicians, and the outlets it created. The mainstay were the instrumentalists and singers chosen from the groups which were signed to the record company, or which it began to create: the Fania Allstars, who were now forever on tour in far-off places. On top of this were the recordings different groups made for the record company which, by 1975, included almost all the bands based in New York. A third service the company provided was matching instrumentalists with outstanding singers who did not have a fixed band.

In the years following the film, 'Salsa', Fania became a gigantic machine for launching and buying up record companies, distributors, and radio stations. In the process, they succeeded in placing their musicians in the mainstream music business. Salsa had thus achieved what it had set out to do: to show that it was more than just 'exotic, Caribbean folklore'.

However, just when everything appeared to be going smoothly, irrational ambitions surfaced, together with two real weaknesses: the Fania Allstars' obsessive desire to conquer US markets which began to distort Latin music and to sap it of its unique life. This tendency was evident in the LP recorded from a disastrous concert at the Yankee Stadium, called 'Latin, Soul, Rock'. It combined Latin music with the latest sounds from the soul and rock world in an attempt to reach as wide an audience as possible – a practice known as 'crossover'. Only '*El Ratón*' (The Mouse), a simple but funny and catchy tune and the very first 'hit' of the salsa boom, saved the whole album. '*El Ratón*' had an electric guitar solo by Jorge Santana (Carlos Santana's brother), and was sung by Cheo Feliciano. The year was 1974.

*Mi gato se está quejando*
*que no puede vacilar*
*si donde quiera que se mete,*
*tu lo sae',*
*su gata lo va buscar*
*De noche brinca la verja*
*que está detrás de mi casa*
*a ver, a ver,*
*a ver si puede fugarse*
*sin que ella lo pueda ver*
*Pero tan pronto está de fiesta*
*Sylvestre, el felino*
*tiene que embalá'a correr.*
*Esto sí es serio mi amigo*
*oye qué lío, pero qué lío se va a formar*
*cuando mi gatito sepa*
*y es tan simple la razón,*
*que el que a su gata le cuenta*
*que el que a su gata le dice*
*es nada más que un ratón,*
*un ratón.*

My cat is complaining
that he doesn't have a chance
wherever he goes
you know
his lady wife goes and finds him.
At night he jumps the fence
at the back of my place
to try and see
if he can get away
without her seeing him
but as soon as he finds some fun
poor Sylvester
has to head out running.
He has a hard time my friend
and there's sure to be trouble
when my cat finds out
the simple reason for it
that the one who tells his wife
the one who gives him away
is none other than a mouse
a mouse.

*El ratón*, version by Cheo Feliciano and the Fania Allstars

The key weakness which the boom demonstrated was the lack of really good salsa composers and arrangers who could keep up with the sales boom without lowering their standards. In 1977-1978, the demand was so great that those musicians capable of something more than the repetitive, undemanding commercial salsa sound simply could not cope. Unfortunately, the Fania promoters did not realise this, as by now they were more concerned with easy money than with the ideals of the 1960s. Their music became a production line for immediate consumption. Some bands accepted the rules of the game imposed by the producers; others had to accept it to fulfil their contracts; a few chose to break free whatever the consequences. The end result was a gradual break-up of Fania, the Allstars and the record company.

This was Fania's big mistake. The company had taken great risks to get its product into the marketplace, and achieved unprecedented results. The company had gambled everything on selling salsa and if it hadn't, salsa would not occupy the position it now does in the history of world music. But Fania went too far. As the Spanish saying goes, it caught the tiger but couldn't handle its skin. Still the party had to go on, and this was by no means the end of salsa music.

*Que nadie discuta mi presencia*
*que no me saquen de mi posición*
*no soy desconocido y a conciencia*
*sigo con paso firme a donde voy*
*soy antillano y le pregono al mundo*
*que la melaza tiene su valor...*

*Me vuelvo loco si discuten mi presencia...*

Don't let anyone ask why I'm here
or try to get rid of me
I'm not nobody and I know
exactly where I intend to go
I'm Caribbean and I'll tell the world
that molasses have their worth...

I go wild if anyone asks what I'm doing here

*Presencia*, version by Justo Betancourt

# 7

# BREAKING WITH TRADITION

## Women and Salsa

*Es cuestión de analizar,*
*mi querido compañero,*
*si vale más un guaguancó*
*que ponerse a sollozar*
*por un amor que te dejó.*
*Es cuestión de comprender*
*la experiencia de la vida*
*sin preguntar al alma*
*qué se va a hacer*
*cuando un amor te abandonó.*
*Y seguir con el mundo hacia adelante*
*y admitir que lo que se fue,*
*se fue.*
*Es cuestión ya de saber,*
*mi querido compañero,*
*no desconfíes, no, no,*
*de la fidelidad de un buen tambor*
*cuando toca un guaguancó.*

The thing to think about
dear friend of mine
is if a guaguancó is worth more
than to sit weeping
over a love that's gone.
The thing is to understand
the experience life brings
without searching your soul
to find out what to do
when love abandons you.

To carry on with things
admitting that what's gone
is gone.
The thing is to know
dear friend of mine
and not to mistrust, no, no
the faithful beat of a true drum
when it plays a guaguanco.

*Vale más un guaguancó*, version by Ray Barreto.

The salsa boom may have commercialised Latin music but it also gave a green light to all those who saw Latin music as a challenge, as was shown by the birth of a company called Latin Percussion in New Jersey. As its name suggests, Latin Percussion aimed at producing the highest quality percussion instruments and catered for many of the great salsa musicians, including Tito Puente.

## Cultural Salsa

The enthusiasm for this new music also led to the creation of the first Latin-Caribbean music school on the whole continent (outside Cuba), the East Harlem Music School. Beginning in 1972 with just 45 students, it can now boast 1,200, who receive bilingual classes in theory, percussion (conga, bongos, timbales), piano, trombone, trumpet, saxophone, flute, guitar, double-bass, singing and dance, without regard to language, sex, or age. This wonderful school, founded and directed by the maestro Johnny Colón and kept afloat thanks to many sacrifices and voluntary contributions, has always aimed to give its students the chance to work as musicians, and to promote Latin culture. But it also uses music to help combat drug addiction. Some of the greatest Latin musicians have shared their knowledge with young musicians in this school.[1]

It was Larry Harlow who realised that the salsa boom should take advantage of all the cultural opportunities it could: in 1973 he staged a salsa opera in New York's Carnegie Hall, based on the rock opera 'Tommy' by the English group The Who. 'Hommy' as the Spanish version was called, had excellent vocalists: Cheo Feliciano, Justo

Betancourt, Pete 'Conde' Rodríguez, Henry Alvarez, Adalberto Santiago, and Junior González. The female part, known as Divine Grace, was played by a former member of the Sonora Matancera, Celia Cruz. At that time, Celia Cruz lived in Mexico and was somewhat removed from the salsa circuit. The version on the record is her first and last, sung without rehearsal or a single mistake or retake.[2] Quite astounding.

Nothing like this had ever been tried in salsa before. The recordings were done part by part, and everyone said that the pianist Larry Harlow was off his head. The orchestra was huge, each singer sang their own lines, nobody knew what was going on. In fact, it wasn't completely original, because it followed the English version quite closely: the London neighbourhood was changed to the Barrio in New York, for example, where a deaf, dumb and blind boy was a genius on the bongo. But all's well that ends well, and the initial pessimism proved unfounded. 'Hommy' was an attempt to give salsa a different connotation: even though it was a product of the Barrio, it could take its place in the world of contemporary music it had to compete with.

The following year, Harlow recorded his famous album '*Salsa*', which included two surprise hits, '*La cartera*' and '*El paso de Encarnación*' – both subtle charanga numbers. Nobody ever imagined that the charanga would make a comeback, especially since salsa bands had split the flute from the violins. The charanga groups which appeared or re-formed as a result of this renewed popularity, such as Broadway, Típica Novel, Ideal, Charanga 76 or América, remained faithful to traditional charanga rhythms, but added contemporary elements.

## Women in the Spotlight

Something important happened in these charanga groups which does not seem to have been noticed. This was the prominent role played by women performers. At every stage in the history of Afro-Cuban and Latin music, women have been striking by their absence, especially as instrumentalists. In these charanga groups, things were different. There are very few studies on the role of women musicians in the Caribbean – in sharp contrast to the incredible number of songs devoted to women, whether ugly, pretty, mulatta, blonde, 'good' or 'evil' in the way they love, and so on.

Ironically, it was the capitalists' concern in pre-revolutionary Cuba to offer tourists variety which first gave women the opportunity to work autonomously. Despite difficulties, women managed to break down the social barriers which had prevented them from taking part in rehearsals or working at night. The most famous of these women performers was María Teresa Vera, lead singer and guitarist of the Sexteto Occidente, who had begun singing at the age of sixteen. Also prominent were Celeste Mendoza, Paulina Alvarez, Rita Montaner, and the still unsurpassable Celia Cruz. In Puerto Rico and Cuba, Myrta Silva was a star, as were the Mexican Toña la Negra or Graciela, who sang for Machito's Big Band. Several all-female groups like Anacaona, Ensueño, or Orbe, also went down in history. And of course in Mexico, Cuba and New York there were the women dancers who choreographed the performances of the mambo groups, and who had been famous ever since the first Latin films.

But when the Latin-Caribbean music scene transferred to New York, women had this shortlived space taken away from them once again. One of the few to succeed was Lupe Victoria Yolí, 'La Lupe', who sang with Tito Puente's band for a number of years. 'La Lupe' was compared to Isadora Duncan for her disregard for social conventions and the show she performed on stage, throwing her shoes or other articles of clothing into the audience. Her voice was harsh, a bit aggressive, but effective:

> *Según tu punto de vista*
> *yo soy la mala.*
> *Vampiresa en tu novela,*
> *la gran tirana.*
> *Cada cual en este mundo,*
> *cuenta el cuento a su manera*
> *y lo hace ver de otro modo*
> *en la mente de cualquiera.*
>
> *Desencadenas en mi*
> *venenosos comentarios,*
> *después de hacerme sufrir*
> *el peor de los calvarios.*

*Según tu punto de vista*
*yo soy la mala.*
*La que te llegó al alma,*
*la gran tirana.*
*Para mí es indiferente*
*lo que sigas comentando,*
*si dice la misma gente*
*que el día que te dejé,*
*fui yo quién salió ganando.*

According to you,
I'm the evil one
the vampire in your novel,
the great tyrant.
Everyone in the world
tells their version of the story
and tries to get their view
into other people's minds.

So you pour on me
your poisonous comments
after putting me through
the worst suffering imaginable.

According to you
I'm the evil one.
The one who touched your soul
the great tyrant.

It's all the same to me
what you go round saying
because everybody agrees
that the day I left you
I came out winning.

*La Tirana*, version by La Lupe

By the mid 1970s, the female presence in the charanga groups
was more obvious. These were not so much Latin women as North
Americans. Nor did they play any instrument other than the essential

flute. What an unforgettable sight it was for those of us who were lucky enough to see one of these women converting air into fire!

The first was Andrea Brachfeld, who surprised everyone when she became part of La Charanga 76, followed by Karen Joseph and Carla Poole. Miryam Stern and Linda Shapiro were virtuosos on the violin, that other indispensable element in any self-respecting charanga line-up. By the end of the 1970s, in San Francisco, there was Rebeca Mauleón, leader, pianist, arranger and singer in a group called Batachanga. Rebeca specialised in experimenting with Afro-Cuban music and thus became closely connected with past and present Cuban musicians.[3] Incidentally, neither salsa nor Afro-Cuban music in general have ever been very successful on the West coast, which makes Rebeca's and Batachanga's efforts all the more praiseworthy.

In more recent years, many young women have tried to enter the world of salsa as instrumentalists or singers, and a number of all-female bands have appeared on the circuit (though their managers have usually been male). Unfortunately, most of these women have given up after only a short time. Why should this be? Two people can answer such a question. Celia Cruz was once asked if she could see anyone following in the footsteps of her own spectacular career. She replied that she had once thought this might be Yolandita Rivera, who sang with the Sonora Ponceña (the best salsa group, together with the Gran Combo, in Puerto Rico): 'but as I understand it, she has had to drop out because one of her children is ill, so how can a woman sing and leave her child like that... Not all women are like me, with no children, so I can travel wherever I like'.[4]

Yolanda did seem to have what it takes to become a great singer. Moreover, she learned a great deal from the professionals in La Ponceña. Papo Lucca, top salsa pianist and leader of the group, told me: 'There were a lot of problems with Yolandita Rivera. She was a married woman, and found it difficult to travel because of her husband and children. We found that in a year we could only count on her for six months, which was no good: it's vital to tour'.[5]

# Celia Cruz

Over sixty years old now, Celia Cruz is still the queen of salsa, the best. On tour after tour, she is always accompanied by her husband Pedro Knight, ex-trumpeter with Sonora Matancera. After Larry Harlow brought her from Mexico to record 'Hommy', Celia stayed on in New York, and became even more popular in the city than she had been in the 1950s with Sonora Matancera. There are few singers who can claim to be the favourite of grandfathers, fathers, and sons simultaneously but Celia is one of them. Even her vociferous opposition to Fidel Castro's government was forgotten by many left-wing militants when they actually saw or heard her perform.

It is difficult to describe Celia, because words don't do her justice. Offstage she is a simple, friendly, disciplined woman; onstage she can whip up a storm capable of blowing everyone and everything away. She began recording with the Sonora, then with Pepe Salamanca, Tito Puente, Johnny Pacheco, Willie Colón, la Ponceña... she was at her best in the kind of line-up that Pacheco had, which was close to that of the Matancera, and enabled her to fuse different styles and generations with great success. She and Héctor Lavoe became the central figures in any Fania concert. With Willie Colón she produced truly classic work, and with Puente she travelled the world, from Paris to Japan. Celia's songs show a clear influence of the polytheistic Afro-Cuban philosophy: by which I mean the worship of many different, opposed gods. Some of her songs are openly anti-Castro:

*Yo nunca perdí la fe ni en el momento peor*
*cuando yo vi con dolor la felicidad que fue*
*lo que llorando dejé y ahora mi vista no alcanza*
*caballerías de labranza, cultivadas extensiones*
*más no me faltan razones pues me sobra la esperanza.*

*Hay siempre caminos para volver,*
*sobran caminos para volver...*

*Tierra mía cómo te extraño*
*nunca me olvido de ti*
*aunque han pasado los años*

*y las cosas han cambiado*
*te juro que mi cariño por ti jamás ha mermado.*
*Y si diosito me llama y por fin no he regresado*
*échame tu bendición, mi tierra,*
*soy tu hija, no he fallado.*

Even in the worst moments I never lost my faith
when painfully I saw that happiness had gone
all I had tearfully left behind and can no longer see
ploughed fields, slopes full of crops
yet still I know I can feel hope.

There are always ways back
so many ways back home...

How much I miss you, my homeland
I've never forgotten you
though the years have gone by
and things have changed
I swear my love for you has never faltered.
And if God calls me before I can return
give me your blessing, land of mine,
I am your daughter, and have never failed you.

*Camino para volver*, version by Celia Cruz with La Sonora
Matancera

At other times, she has surprised people with songs that have said
things in a way no political organisation has managed to. Take this
appeal for Latin unity:

*Latinos en Estados Unidos*
*ya casi somos una nación*
*venimos de la América india,*
*del negro, del español,*
*en nuestra mente migrante*
*a veces hay confusión*
*pero no hay quién nos engañe*
*el alma y el corazón*
*porque vivimos soñando*

*volver al sitio de honor*

*Latinos en Estados Unidos*
*vamos a unirnos, vamos unirnos...*

*En la unión está la fuerza*
*y al pueblo respetan y le dan valor*
*no dejes que te convenzan*
*que no se pierda el idioma español*

Latins of the USA
we're almost a nation by now
we come from America that's
indian, black, and Spanish,
in our migrant minds
sometimes there is confusion
but no-one can fool
our souls or our hearts
because we constantly dream
of regaining our rightful place

Latins of the USA
let's unite, unite...

Unity gives strength
and gives a people respect and value
don't let anyone persuade you
to abandon your Spanish language...

*Latinos en Estados Unidos*, version by Celia Cruz

   What could be more demagogic? Celia's message somehow got through to all the sons and daughters of Latin immigrants who were unwilling to learn Spanish due to the pressures of cultural assimilation and felt ashamed of their parents' origins.

# 8

## SALSA POLITICA

### A Colombian's Story

I come from Cali, Colombia. I am the product of hardworking
parents but I also belong to my neighbourhood in Cali, its streets,
its inhabitants. That's where I grew up and learnt all I had to learn,
for good or for bad. Every night as we clustered round a transistor
radio on the street corner, salsa entered our lives without so much
as a by your leave, and we accepted it; the music was like a woman
who makes you fall in love with her without you realising it, and
once she has you, she never lets you go.

That street corner brought us everything: pachanga, the
Matamoros, Ricardo Ray, the Sonora Matancera, all the groups. On
Fridays or Saturdays – both if we could – we would buy a bottle of
cheap brandy or maybe rum. Just to raise the temperature a little,
you understand. As you can imagine, we became the main topic of
conversation for every nosy old lady in the neighbourhood. Some
mothers forbade their daughters to say anything more than hello to
us. But just because we weren't the kind of boys who talked about
maths or geography or went to bed early, that doesn't meant to say
we were bad boys. In fact, we managed to study at school *and* paint
the town red.

It was in the early 1970s that I began to notice the first bridges
being built across the gulf in our knowledge. Those of us Latins
who lived in the rest of the continent knew little of the lives of our
fellow Latins resident in the US. From the scanty, manipulated news
we received, it seemed impossible to believe that our fellow
countrymen were dying in Vietnam, returning in coffins or as
madmen, fighting on behalf of a flag and a western civilisation which
in many other respects wanted nothing to do with them. Meanwhile
in New York, the few who heard anything about the growing guerrilla
struggles in Colombia, El Salvador, Guatemala or Nicaragua, were

left cold by the news, as they were by the rise and fall of the bloody dictatorships in the Southern Cone countries.

The same thing had happened in music, which is why the 'bridges' built by the Fania company were so important. Firstly, Fania managed to win over the old 'veterans' of the Latin music world to the new salsa sound, while at the same time the young musicians learnt to value and respect all that the maestros of the recent past had created. Secondly, Fania succeeded in 'packaging' the various Caribbean and Latin American sounds for a mainstream audience while also introducing the experimental sounds created by the 'newyorlatins' to the rest of the continent.

Stimulated initially by the film, 'Our Latin Thing', the first hesitant salsa bands began to emerge in various Latin American countries. Although they closely followed New York models, these bands added their own grains of sand to the expansion of salsa. Radio stations devoted to salsa started to appear, while others dedicated a daily slot to the new music; the Latin American programme controllers were yielding to the pressure of an expectant public who wanted to keep pace with the latest developments on the salsa music scene. The boom in salsa music was so big that even the mass media could not ignore it. Press reports were often disparaging, but nevertheless contributed to the spread of the salsa phenomenon.

## Oscar d'León

In the mid-1970s, at a time when reggae musicians were taking planes and boats from Jamaica to destinations across the world, a young Venezuelan singer, Oscar d'León, and his modest group began to make ripples. They were interesting for two reasons. The first was that they played salsa; the second that they played it not in New York or Puerto Rico, but in their own country, which until then had been seen merely as a place where New York groups could land fat contracts. The oil boom was partly responsible for this: with increased migration from the countryside to cities such as Caracas or Maracaibo, more people were driven into the shanty towns which were salsa's natural surroundings.

The band was called Dimensión Latina and played a classic New York sound, but Oscar d'León's gift for improvisation, coupled with his brilliant bass playing, marked the band out from the rest. Like many other rising salsa stars before him, Oscar soon left Dimensión Latina and set up on his own, astounding everyone with his reworking of '*La Mata Siguaraya*' by Beny Moré.

To replace him, Dimensión Latina turned to the first singer with the Gran Combo, Andy Montañez. Although they paid him a fortune, it was not enough to check Oscar d'León's rising popularity. First d'León toured Latin America, then he leapt across to Spain, where he was the first salsa musician to fill the Plaza Mayor in Madrid. He was also the first Latin to sign a contract with the BBC for his music to be played all over Europe. He has appeared in Caracas and New York, London, Paris, and Tokyo; not forgetting Lima, Managua or Cali. He is without doubt the top son singer of today.

In Venezuela there were other interesting bands such as Nelson y sus Estrellas (Nelson and his Allstars) who were very popular in Colombia, the Trabuco Venezolano, a kind of Allstars band, and some time later the Sonero Clásico del Caribe, which was interesting because as its name suggests, it returned to the son in its original form. Formed in 1977, the Trabuco attempted to apply the lessons of Fania, but without falling into the trap of over-simplifying the music as the Allstars had.

A similar approach was taken by Grupo Folclórico y Experimental Newyorkino, which despite its short life was perhaps the best of all these innovative bands. There were also the Puerto Rico Allstars (PRAS), and the Supertípica de Estrellas, which played in the charanga tradition. But none of these bands could rival what the Fania Allstars had achieved, because they did not reach a very wide public.

The only serious challengers were the Estrellas SAR, led by Roberto Torres, nicknamed 'the wayfarer', who was honoured by the US Senate in January 1991 because his music 'has helped unite the world'.[1] First formed in 1979, SAR mostly got together musicians and singers of Cuban origin (for example, Mario 'Papaíto' Muñoz, 'Chocolate' Armenteros, Linda Leyda, Alfredo Valdez). But most of their songs were old Cuban themes, lacking any originality in their arrangements.

Earlier I mentioned Venezuela, a country which played a key role in reuniting salsa musicians with Cuban musicians still living in Cuba, because Venezuela was one of the first countries to timidly lift the embargo. It was here and in Panama that the first evidence could be heard of the son's continuing existence in Cuba. A kind of cultural exchange developed amidst a mixture of expectation, fears, feigned indifference, and happy discoveries; the rediscovery of two identical worlds which since 1960 had been so near yet so far from each other. These meetings and exchanges continued fairly regularly in various Latin American and European countries from the mid-seventies onwards.

## Music in Castro's Cuba

So what had happened to music in Cuba itself during those 15 years without contact with the outside world? Well, people were still enjoying themselves, but there were different political needs. It is true that for many years the State's priorities were centred around a highly politicised music that became known as the Nueva Trova, where the message was more important than the rhythm. This music was especially appreciated in Chile and Argentina. It may have been that the authorities wished to break away from the stereotype of Cuba and prostitution under the Batista government, and for this reason there was not the same support for dance music.

This was the first stage. After that there was a period of rock, and even of disco music. But by the mid-1970s there was complete support for the rumba, which produced a lot of good music scarcely known outside the island because of the increasingly harsh blockade. Cuba never stopped making music to dance to. That would have been impossible, because Cubans are stuffed full of rhythms and are perhaps the most musical of all nationalities, as an astounded CBS TV director noted when he visited the island in the late 1970s. The Cubans' musicality needed no outlet or support: its inventions and musical innovations such as the guaguancó, the danzón, the chachacha, the mambo, the guajira and the one and only son have provided the foundations on which the whole edifice of salsa was built.

But the Cubans did not stop there. They went on creating: the *chaonda*, the *paca*, *mozambique*, *pilón*, *songo*, and on and on. As I have mentioned, this music is barely known outside the island because of the difficulties of winning contracts or getting proper distribution in the face of the imperialist blockade.

The blockade is also responsible for the poor recording and production possibilities for this Cuban music – as anyone who has listened to a record 'Made in Cuba' can testify. Yet there is no denying that intense, serious and creative work is being done in Cuba. What about Los Van Van, Son 14, La Aragón, Orquesta Ritmo Oriental, Elio Revé, or Celina Gonzáles, to name only those known internationally? What about the virtuoso sounds of Irakere? In 1979, the organisers of the Grammy awards could not go on ignoring the obvious, and gave an award to Irakere's leader Jesús 'Chucho' Valdez, one of the world's best pianists. Irakere won this recognition for their explosive mixture of jazz, classical sounds, rock and Cuban rhythms. While using their Afro-Cuban roots as a basis, Irakere creates music that is full of contemporary harmonies.

The Cuban musical spirit comes from everday life. They are always ready to celebrate life, whatever the economic difficulties imposed on them from abroad. And their creativity has not suffered with the departure of some musicians who still found themselves dazzled by the golden dream of capitalism.

The political triumph that Cuba won on the night of 28 December 1978 is still vivid in my mind. That was the occasion when, in New York's Lincoln Center, Rafael Lay announced to a large audience: 'Ladies and gentlemen, here with us tonight: the Orquesta Aragón from Cuba'. However much the anti-Castroists tried to play the occasion down, insulting the group and more or less forbidding people to go to the concert, countless people did attend. It may have been that they went to see if the longest-lasting of Cuban groups could still play. There was more than just good music in the air that night.

I have already mentioned that Batachanga took advantage of a slight relaxation of the embargo. Even more prominent in this respect was the Típica 73. Their music was based on Afro-Cuban roots, and though they did not secure the popularity they deserved, their sustained efforts and polished presentation made people sit up and listen and tap their feet in approval.

It was the Típica 73 who fulfilled what had been the dream of many groups: they toured Cuba, becoming the first group based in the United States to do so for twenty years. The band was made up of Latins from several different countries, including Cuban exiles, which gave a special significance to what they themselves called 'a cultural exchange'. The record they produced is unique, drawing as it does on contributions from such outstanding Cuban musicians as

Felix Chapottín, who plays a sensational trumpet, and Tata Güinez, unequalled anywhere in the world on the congas.

When the Típica returned to the United States, they came up against a problem which has affected many others since. The Cuban exiles decreed a 'Miami punishment' against them for daring to go to the island. In other words, they established a boycott, refusing to buy, distribute or give airtime on the many radio stations they controlled, to any group that had been to Cuba. This boycott has now spread to other cities in the United States, with serious economic consequences for any such group. Even though he denies it, it seems that Oscar d'León had to promise he would never return to the Varadero Festival. Only the Fania Allstars, who had a solid enough structure not to worry about these things, were able to defy the ban.

## The Left discovers salsa

It was towards the end of the 1970s that President Jimmy Carter visited the Latin Barrio in New York, and was able to see for himself the dreadful conditions people lived in there. This unexpected visit, made with obvious electoral intent, finally led the big transnational record companies to realise the importance of the neglected market of some twenty million Latins, with an even greater number of possible buyers in Latin America, the Caribbean, Europe, and elsewhere in the world. One of these companies was negotiating with Fania for the rights to distribute its salsa records worldwide; another signed up Eddie Palmieri, who in 1975 and 1976 had won two Grammy awards – the 'Oscars' of the music world. Palmieri was the first Latin involved in salsa to receive one of these coveted awards – although in fact it was more in recognition of all that he had done in Latin-jazz. The following year Mongo Santamaría won one, and then in 1978 it was Tito Puente's turn: both for their efforts in Latin jazz. It was only several years later that the Grammy organisers put aside their prejudices against musicians who specialised in salsa.

It was also around this period that left-wing intellectuals and politicians began to accept salsa *en masse*, though not all of it. Due to their narrow view of how ordinary people should enjoy themselves, their first encounters were with the masters of Latin jazz, to whom most salsa aficionados were indifferent. Until then, it had been extremely rare to see any left-wing intellectual dancing in the same place as a worker; hence the joke: 'If the police wanted to arrest any left-wingers in this bar, they would only need one patrol-car, and there'd still be room left over'. Perhaps this is why it is only very recently that these people have begun to realise the possibilities of using salsa to help organise in the communities that enjoy it so much.

It was only in 1979, thanks to the songs '*Plástico*' and '*Pedro Navaja*' recorded by Willie Colón and Ruben Blades from Panama on their LP '*Siembra*' that the Left totally accepted the new music. This epoch-making record, the biggest seller in the whole history of Latin Caribbean music, brought people from all social classes flocking to salsa. Today, many on the Left are still discovering what they've been missing all these years.

> *Ella era una chica plástica, de ésas que veo por ahí;*
> *de ésas que cuando se agitan, sudan Chanel Number Three,*
> *que sueñan casarse con un doctor*
> *pues él puede mantenerlas mejor,*
> *no le hablan a nadie si no es su igual,*
> *a menos que sea fulano de tal.*
> *Son lindas, esbeltas, de buen vestir,*
> *de mirada esquiva y falso reir.*
>
> *El era un muchacho plástico, de ésos que veo por ahí;*
> *con la peinilla en la mano y cara de yo no fui;*
> *que por tema en conversación*
> *discuten que marca de carro es mejor;*
> *de los que prefieren el no comer*
> *por las apariencias que hay que tener*
> *para andar elegantes y así poder una chica plástica recoger.*
>
> *Era una pareja plástica, de ésas que veo por ahí:*
> *él pensando siempre en dinero, ella en la moda en París;*
> *aparentando lo que no son,*
> *viviendo en un mundo de pura ilusión,*
> *diciendo a su hijo de cinco años:*
> *no juegues con niños de color extraño;*
> *ahogados en deudas para mantener su status social*
> *en boda o coctel...*

She was a plastic woman, like many you can see
the kind who when they move, sweat Chanel Number Three
who dream of marrying a doctor
to buy them all they wish for
who only speak to those the same
unless it's someone with a name.
they're pretty, elegant and slender too
their laugh is hollow and their eyes avoid you.

He was a plastic man, like many you can see;
comb in hand, a face that says 'it wasn't me'.
All they ever seem to discuss
is which sort of car is best
those who prefer not to eat any food
so they can look as they think they should
to be elegant and pick up a plastic mate.

They were a plastic couple, like many you can see:
he always thinking of money, she of fashion in Paris;
pretending to be what they are not
living in a world of illusion,
telling their little five-year-old
not to play with coloured kids
drowning in debt to keep up their status
at weddings or at cocktail parties

*Plástico,* version by Willie Colón and Ruben Blades

It was a long time before anyone recognised that salsa had always
been about something, that most of the salsa songs had something
to say, and were not just about nothing in particular. Of course, not
everyone had the same view of what a political message was. Few
of our musicians have been through further education; only Blades
is a lawyer with left-wing university politics behind him. Poets like
him who can write whole novels in each of their songs are few and
far between.

But many salsa artists have had a message to get across. The crux
is that this has not been their only aim. What about the way Cheo

Feliciano has interpreted his Latin American 'family', or the songs
written by Bobby Capó or Alonso Tite Curet, the black Puerto Rican
who has been a tireless guide for so many younger musicians? For
years, even the Eddie Palmieri of the early 1970s was not recognised,
when he wrote songs that clearly defined the position of the
Newyorlatin in North American society. He sang it in the ghastly
Sing Sing jail, in front of countless black, Latin, Irish, and Italian
prisoners:

*No, no, no,*
*no me trates así (coro)*

*La libertad, caballero,*
*no me la quites a mí.*
*Pero que mira, pero mira,*
*pero mira que también soy humano*
*y fue aquí donde nací*

*Económicamente,*
*económicamente esclavo de ti*

*Esclavo de ti, esclavo de ti,*
*esclavo de ti caballero*
*pero que va, tú no me engañas,*
*tú no me engañas a mí.*

*La libertad, lógico,*
*la libertad, lógico,*
*la libertad, lógico...*

No, no, no,
don't treat me this way (chorus)

don't take away
my freedom from me.
Listen, just listen
listen; I'm human too
and I was born here

Economically
economically your slave

Your slave, your slave,
your very own slave
but anyway, you can't fool me
you can't fool me

Freedom, of course,
freedom, of course,
freedom, of course...

*La libertad, lógico*, version by Eddie Palmieri

## Eddie Palmieri

Palmieri got where he was from being the leader of two bands, both of them experimental. One of them was a salsa band; the other played Afro-North American music. They shifted imperceptibly between salsa, jazz and blues. Palmieri was an excellent soloist born in the Bronx, and unusually, had been to music school. Relying heavily on the creativity of his trombonist Barry Rogers, he took the devotees of vanguard music into salsa, leading a modest group called La Perfecta.

The trombones in La Perfecta had none of the conventional elegance of the big bands. Here, their arrangements were sharp, harsh, aggressive, even violent. They brought with them the feelings of the Barrio, the violence of the Young Lords or the demands of the Black Panthers. Palmieri also used the son as the rhythmic base for his improvisations, and this was taken up by later groups, as the son could still accommodate all kinds of experiments and remain the pre-eminent musical form. Pacheco was another musician who was quick to realise this.

Eddie Palmieri did not seem interested in the drive to commercialise salsa; nor was he particularly concerned about creating tunes that could be danced to. This meant that as the salsa boom grew, his music was listened to by a small minority who we could perhaps classify as the newly emerging 'intellectuals' of salsa.

Others claim that after Barry Rogers broke from the group, Palmieri's sound became repetitive and lacked innovation.

## Willie, Héctor and Ruben

The same could not be said of Willie Colón, known as *El Malo* (the Bad Boy) or *El Diablo* (the Devil). Though he was a great innovator, he never forgot the dancer, and this made his music among the most popular of the decade. He was less interested in jazz than in Puerto Rican, Brazilian, Colombian and Panamanian folklore. Although still a youngster in the late seventies, his aggressive sound got better and more contemporary by the day. Rather than any direct socio-political message, most of his work gave a convincing portrayal of an urban society in a cheerful, popular language.

Earlier, Willie had helped his former singer, Héctor Lavoe become one of the most successful performers of the salsa boom. He was also the mastermind of a successful partnership with Ruben Blades. One day Willie and Ruben happened to meet in the Fania offices. Blades was not very happy, because although he had a singer's contract, he was being used as the office dogsbody, which is what he was doing when he ran into Colón. Thanks to their meeting, many things changed in salsa. And without that chance meeting, Blades would never have got where he is today.

After arriving in New York from Panama in the 1960s, Blades teamed up with the former king of boogaloo, Pete Rodríguez. In 1970 they recorded the song '*Juan González*' together, which tells the story of the death of a guerrilla in an army ambush. The record made little impact in New York, because the public was unable to relate to the theme, whilst in several Latin American countries it was censored for its subversive content. In 1974, Blades contributed to the best salsa record ever made by Ray Barreto, the LP entitled '*Barreto*'. But it was not until he joined up with Willie and Lavoe in 1975 to sing '*El bueno, el malo y el feo*' (The Good, the Bad, and the Ugly) that Blades came into his own. In 1977 he worked with Lavoe on the LP '*Metiendo Mano*' (Putting Your Hand To It), and sang '*Juan Pachanga*', the immediate predecessor to the world-famous '*Pedro Navaja*', on a record produced by the maestro Loui Ramírez and accompanied by the Allstars.

'Pedro Navaja' is the story of a thief, a prostitute and a drunkard. The thief, Pedro, who is graphically described in the song, mortally wounds the prostitute with a knife as he is trying to rob her. She unexpectedly manages to shoot him with her revolver, and both of them fall to the ground dead. At this point the drunkard, who knows them both, stumbles over their bodies, and is able to make off with their belongings, singing as he does so: 'la vida te da sorpresas, sorpresas te da la vida'. (Life is full of surprises, surprises there are in life.)

With this song, Blades broke with all the elements that had become traditional in salsa: rather than singing, he was telling a story. He wasn't the first to use these kind of words, but he was the first to make his songs into mini-novels in which the entire social climate of a typical Latin city was crystallised. With 'Pedro Navaja', Blades brought a new popularity to intellectual, poetic songs in a salsa mould.

In the 1980s, Blades separated from Willie but continued to flourish, although his style remained uniquely his own. Meanwhile, Colón himself began to sing, experimenting with a mixture of traditional and electronic instruments. He was still one of the best, and remained 'a socio-political animal active in the community', as he once defined himself.

> (...) La droga!
> te vira la vida al revés,
> estás entregado y no ves
> lo bueno que hay en otras cosas
> Droga! por todo, por nada
> y por qué en lo negativo caés
> si la vida te ofrece otras cosas.
>
> Pana! olvida la droga
> porque te estás acabando
> y no ves que la vida
> te ofrece otras cosas.
> Droga! ponle ya punto porque
> te vas a morir sin saber
> que tu vida merece otras cosas.
>
> Droga!

*De lejos te miro y se ve*
*que empujas aquella pared*
*buscando una vida sabrosa.*
*Droga! Te vira la vida al revés,*
*te metes pa'entro y no gozas.*
*Para qué tú estás en eso,*
*el cuello no es para soga...*

(...) Drugs!
they turn your life upside down,
you're hooked and cannot see
how good other things can be.
Drugs! they're all or nothing
why fall into a trap like that
when life has other things to offer.

Friend! forget drugs
they're destroying you
and you cannot see
life has other things to offer.
Drugs! Put a stop to them or else
you'll die without ever knowing
your life deseves something better.

Drugs!
From far off I watch you and can tell
you're banging your head against that wall
because you want a better life.
Drugs! they turn your life upside down,
you turn in on yourself and find no pleasure
why have you got mixed up in them
our necks weren't made for ropes...

*Careta*, version by Ismael Miranda

# 9

# THE NINETIES

## Salsa-erótica, Merengue and Cumbia

*Déjame presentar al grupo mío*
*todos los miembros son chéveres,*
*aunque ellos son todos japoneses*
*pero tocan la salsa sabrosa.*
*El director comenzó a tocar bongó*
*porque le gusta la Sonora Ponceña y el Gran Combó.*
*El trompetista comenzó a tocar música latina*
*porque le gustaba el señor 'Perico';*
*no importa de donde sean,*
*ellos pueden tocar y bailar*
*no importa de donde sean,*
*ellos tienen ritmo y corazón.*

Allow me to present this group of mine
all of them are great people
even though they're all Japanese
they play wonderful salsa.
The leader began to play the bongo
because he likes the Sonora Ponceña and the Gran Combo.
The trumpeter began to play Latin music
because he liked Mister 'Perico';
it doesn't matter where they're from
they can play and sing
it doesn't matter where they're from
they have rhythm and a heart.

*Salsa caliente del Japón*, Orquesta La Luz del Japón.

To hear a salsa lover talking about 'his' or 'her' salsa is to listen to a chauvinist, to the proud owner of the rhythm and the flavour of the music. A salsa lover talks as if it were a matter of life and death: 'just look and listen, concentrate on the way he's playing the timbal, listen to the maracas, and see how softly the bongo comes in... get ready for the trumpets...isn't it incredible?' I've seen people looking idiotic, almost ashamed of themselves, as they struggled to hear and 'see' what they were supposed to, without daring to take their eyes off the salsa fan in his or her agitated trance. Take this salsa fanatic from Cali:

'When I'm dancing salsa, I let it take me over and penetrate every inch of my body. Sometimes it drives me to tears: it's just so electric when the band starts playing, and then there are those tear-jerking lyrics, reminding me of unforgettable moments. I just love sharing every inch of the floor with my partner, and competing with other couples to prove we're the best. I'm a salsa fanatic, and I don't mind admitting it. To dance salsa you need a partner and lots of people around you – people who feel the same way as you do about it. I could write a book about all the things a young Latin woman has to invent or put up with so that she can go dancing of an evening. Not even our partners know much about that. Nowadays dancers don't bother to show off their steps like they used to. That's because of the kind of salsa you hear these days. In the past, you really had to know how to perform; you and your partner had to show what your feet and your body could do. That's what it was like here in Cali, Colombia, but I think it must have been the same in Puerto Rico, New York, Caracas, or anywhere else'.

What has become of salsa in recent years? Firstly, the new generation has got used to a new kind of soft music, so that they no longer seem to know how to move properly, as salsa dancers used to; and you have to choose carefully if you want to find somewhere where the music doesn't all sound exactly the same after the third tune. Those of us who consider ourselves the real salsa lovers have had to put up with the assault of a rosy-erotic-salsa, specially designed for a kind of tropical Julio Iglesias. But no evil lasts forever, and no true salsa fan will allow it to.

The current situation seems to have arisen from the excessive way in which salsa has been commercialised, to an extent that has destroyed all experimentation or creativity. The interplay of instruments has been lost; and the difficult but wonderful art of son singing has been cast aside and forgotten. Nor do the songs have the characteristic references to events or gossip from the barrio nowadays. Instead, the salsa businessmen (those merchants of taste) offer us clumsy passion and cheap eroticism, in quantities similar to the number of bombs dropped on Iraq a few years ago. They have applied an old formula which overlooks creativity but is intended to secure access to new social classes. As far as salsa is concerned, if we consider quality and identity rather than the lining of some people's pockets, the cure may have turned out to be almost worse than the disease.

There have been two stages to this disease. The first of these set in towards the end of the 1980s, when that excellent arranger, producer and musician Loui Ramírez (who recently died) and his group Noches Calientes wrote salsa versions of songs by well-known Spanish ballad singers. These caused a sensation among Latin dancers, because they were generally well done, and the voice of the group's singer, Ray de la Paz, was well suited to this kind of song. They were gentle but interesting songs, with good arrangements and words. When the record companies saw how well these songs by Noches Calientes went down, they began to demand this kind of music all the time. So began the era of salsa ballads.

## Salsa Erótica

Bringing ballads into the dance halls was nothing new, but previously they had only been played sporadically. As far back as I can remember, there have been ballads among the dance tunes, encouraging the first dreams of our adolescent love. Do you remember '*Volare*', which won the San Remo Festival in Italy, sung by Doménico Modugno? That was the most immediate predecessor of a ballad adapted to Caribbean rhythms, thanks to the incredible percussionist Rafael Cortijo, unfortunately now deceased, who really made it fly in 1960.[1] Bands ranging from Tito Rodríguez to the Gran Combo also used love lyrics in their salsa tunes, often with excellent results. But they were just another element of their performance. What happened after Loui's success was a different matter altogether.

By the end of the 1980s, the prominent themes in salsa veered from the rosy to the red, when the people behind the Conjunto Chaney in Puerto Rico decided to launch erotic salsa, soon to be dubbed *salsa-bed* by a knowing public. At least this new fashion meant there was some attempt at being original again, because they had to think of compositions based around sex.

Throughout the history of Afro-Caribbean music, and Latin music in general, love themes have always played an important part. Usually things were spelled out clearly enough, in a popular language. But this new eroticism had little to do with the Latin way of love-making, because our art of loving has always taught us the importance of reciprocal feelings in desire, of the need for some love or affection: and these were absent from this new fashion. What is offered here is merely the female body for consumption. That was why I was so pleased when Cheo Feliciano sang:

*(...) Tú le pediste que se desnudara*
*después que no se quite la ropa*
*luego decidiste que te devorara*
*ya la estás volviendo loca.*
*No te das cuenta como ella te ama,*
*no te das cuenta que ella es mucho más*
*y solamente haces como aquél que llega,*
*come y luego se va.*

*Dices que fuiste segundo en su vida*
*cuando volaban en sábanas blancas*
*y hasta lograste que se olvidara*
*de aquella prenda teñida.*
*Y que de todos eres el mejor,*
*le dices a esa hermosa mujer,*
*que para ti ella sólo significa*
*aquel viejo motel.*

*Cuántas cosas le vas a decir,*
*y que se quite la ropa,*
*que no se la quite,*

*que to devore otra vez,*
*muchacho, pero cuántas cosas.*

*Que seas el primero, el segundo*
*o tercero en su vida no importa,*
*tú sólo la ves sin ropa.*
*Ella te ama y quiere que la mimes,*
*que le des un cariñito,*
*que le digas que es hermosa.*

*Ahora quieres cabalgar su cuerpo*
*como un caballito, como potranca sabrosa.*
*Dale un besito y dile que es hermosa,*
*que tú la amas, que es especial y preciosa...*

(...) You asked her to strip off
then to keep her clothes on
then you wanted her to devour you,
can't you see you're driving her mad?
Can't you see that she loves you,
can't you see she's much more than that
while you act like someone who drifts in
eats his fill and leaves.

You claim you were the second man in her life
as you rolled around in white sheets
you even managed to make her forget
that stain on her clothes.
You are the best of all
you boast to that beautiful woman,
although all she means to you
is that run-down motel.

How much more are you going to ask,
that she take her clothes off,
that she keep them on
that she devour you again
how much more?

115

What does it matter if you're first
or second or third in her life?
You only see her with no clothes on.
She loves you and wants you to be kind
wants you to show her some affection
to tell her she's beautiful.

Now you want to ride her
like a horse, like a little mare.
Give her a kiss and tell her she's beautiful,
that you love her, that's she's really special...

*Cuántas cosas*, version by Cheo Feliciano

Since most of the son singers who had any kind of reputation refused to have anything to do with this new trend, a load of new singers suddenly sprang from nowhere – overnight heroes with good looks but little or no experience of life. All that was needed, it seemed, to make a lie come true was a decent recording studio and a businessman who could buy you spots in the media. This kind of promotion was known as 'Payola' [2] and was based on methods learnt from North American and European record companies.

## Salsa Puertorriqueña

It was with this new boom in ballad and erotic salsa that Puerto Rico re-established itself at the centre of salsa production in the Americas. This in itself is praiseworthy, as it was the island's sons and daughters who had contributed most to salsa in New York, both before and during the boom. It was simply unfortunate that Puerto Rico was now spearheading something of such little value, although the musicians were hardly to blame for that. And it should be recognised that despite this new craze for highly commercialised salsa, there are still some excellent bands in Puerto Rico who can play with true style. The pressure the Latin public has brought to bear on the bands to play real salsa has been essential in maintaining the music's links with its roots.

In Puerto Rico, the salsa musicians face other challenges. It is well-known that Puerto Rican radio, newspapers and television prioritise rock music, and seek to diminish the social role that salsa plays in offering a sense of identity for ordinary people on the island. There is no respect or proper promotion of their popular culture. It sounds incredible in a country where even the stones sing, but it is true: the musicians themselves admit that although salsa music is played in some four hundred town celebrations on the island, it is more appreciated in other countries than in Puerto Rico.[3]

To give but a few examples: it is only recently that a salsa concert could be put on in the Centro de Bellas Artes (Fine Arts Centre) in the capital, San Juan; the government and the middle classes were hotly opposed to a concert hall in this complex being named after Rafael Cortijo, claiming that this mulatto musician had no education; no proper state support is provided for any research, seminars, or conferences on salsa. There is clearly a social and political dimension to this problem when one considers the incessant attempts to smother Puerto Rico in North American culture. In many ways, it is amazing that salsa has been able to resist and survive at all, in the face of so much pressure and imported trends.[4]

## Salsa is tamed

Looking beyond Puerto Rico, two explanations have been put forward to try and explain what has happened to salsa. The first of these sees it as part of the worldwide decadence we are witnessing, in which the increasing atomisation of societies and the manipulation of the mass media have led to the distortion of traditional values and customs.[5] The other view is that it is a consequence of the excessive amount of violence in the world today and people's preference for undemanding music that will help them relax, or for music they can listen to while they're talking or reading, without losing their concentration.[6] Maybe real salsa music is just too exciting: it shakes the dance floor, not to mention the dancers' bodies and it makes you incapable of keeping still.

Some people claim that salsa's hour of perestroika has arrived. This may sound comical but what can be said is that the current trend in salsa music has been a powerful challenge to the aggressive instruments, the impetuous sounds, the get-up-and-dance urge that are all present in traditional salsa. These elements represented the libertarian ideals and cultural pride of large sectors of Latin American society. It is interesting that the new salsa trends have come to the fore in the 1990s, the same decade in which attempts at social transformation in Nicaragua, El Salvador, Peru and Colombia have been attacked and discredited. It has coincided with the years of 'forgiving and forgetting' decreed by governments which practised state terror on their citizens in recent history. Double doses of cheap musical opium have accompanied the discourse on reconciliation and peace which the centres of power have imposed on the poor, in exchange for free markets and 'the American way of life'.

## The Dominican Republic and merengue

In tandem with this erotic salsa, merengue has burst onto the scene. Some people claim that this musical creation from the Dominican Republic is quite simply salsa; others see it as such a close relative that salsa bands have included some merengue songs in their repertoire. The truth is that merengue has a different style, with a flat one-two rhythm, which is straightforward and easy to dance to. That is why it is such a challenge to salsa nowadays.

If we look at the way it became so massively popular both in the cities of the Dominican Republic and elsewhere, we find once again that it is an example of the constant interconnection between music and politics. In the 1930s, the complicated drum rhythms of the Dominican countryside, which are the basis of merengue, were persecuted in various ways by Leonidas Trujillo's dictatorship. His government was intent on 'whitewashing' the countryside and its culture, in order to get rid of any African influences or any similarity with the poor, black culture of neighbouring Haiti.

In 1965, the United States invaded the Dominican Republic, on the pretext of stamping out a revolt by supposedly Communist young officers, who were massively supported by the population. Throughout the occupation by 35,000 marines, popular music was part and parcel of the Dominicans' resistance effort. Merengue, which popped up in all the towns as a means of self-defence, came under attack. This was particularly true of a song by the young Cuco Valoy, who already stood out because of his completely shaven head.

Any jukebox playing '*Páginas gloriosas*' was destroyed, and the bar around it too, because this song became the anthem of resistance.

*En los pueblos gloriosos como el nuestro*
*la libertad se marchita pero no muere.*
*Es un árbol que en las secas entristece*
*pero vuelve y retoña en primavera.*
*porque los hombres de mi patria no se humillan,*
*son muy grandes y machos para rendirse...*

*Maldito sea el soldado*
*que obedece al superior*
*para asesinar a la patria.*
*Maldito sea el soldado*
*que le da la espalda al pueblo*
*para seguir a unos pocos.*
*Y maldito sea el extranjero*
*que sin razón y sin derecho*
*abusa de un pueblo ajeno.*
*Por eso digo en voz dura*
*como soy hijo del pueblo,*
*a estas bestias asesinas*
*mil veces malditas sean...*

In glorious lands like ours
freedom may wither but never dies.
It's a tree which suffers during droughts
but returns with fresh shoots in Spring.
The men of my land won't be humbled
they are too great and brave to surrender...

A curse on the soldier
who obeys an officer
and kills his own nation.
A curse on the soldier
who turns his back on the people
to follow a handful.
And a curse on the foreigner
who with no reason or right
attacks another people.

119

That's why I say in my ringing voice
the voice of a son of the people
that these murdering beasts
be a thousand times cursed.

*Páginas gloriosas,* version by Cuco Valoy

Merengue has clearly benefited from the declining appeal of salsa. From the mid-1980s onwards, it was plain that more and more people, especially those who wanted to dance, were listening to merengue. There is concrete evidence of this in Puerto Rico and New York, where merengue bands earn considerably more than their salsa counterparts: Patrulla 15, Fernando Villalona and Los Hermanos Rosario earn between seven and nine thousand dollars per concert, whereas the Gran Combo, arguably the most popular salsa band, never manages to earn more than seven thousand. Many other well-known salsa bands have to make do with four thousand dollars.[7] Another indication of merengue's popularity is that the same transnational company which promotes Michael Jackson also works for the merengue singer, Juan Luis Guerra. No other Latin artist has ever commanded such a publicity machine.

## Juan Luis Guerra

Let's concentrate for a moment on Juan Luis Guerra and his band 4.40 (which takes its name from the frequency that its instruments are tuned at). Guerra is a composer, arranger, producer, and singer who has studied music both in the Dominican Republic and the United States, and has been able to combine this theoretical knowledge with merengue and other popular rhythms from his country, such as the *bachata*, a Caribbean bolero which is sung and danced to in the north of the Dominican Republic. Although he formed his band in 1985, it was only in 1990 that he became known throughout the American continent and in Europe. His first big hits were '*Bilirrubina*', '*Burbujas de amor*' (Bubbles of love) and '*Ojalá que llueva café*' (Let's hope it rains coffee). Even he himself has found it hard to explain his success: 'perhaps it's because of the many musical references in our music, which the public recognise because they sound familiar. For example, our songs are full of the

Beatles, but the audiences don't consciously realise it. The way we use lyrics is different to the Latin tradition too. It is rare in Latin music for songs to have a message, whether it's about feelings, love or politics. Perhaps that's what people like. My music has a double intention: to make people dance, and to make them think'.

It is true that many of Juan Luis Guerra's songs are based on the social and political situation that the people of the Dominican Republic and the rest of the continent face in their daily lives. 'In the Dominican Republic we have nothing but problems. There's no electricity, and there are often shortages of water, food and even in education... none of this will be solved without real change. As a musician, I am responsible to my own people and to those of the rest of Latin America. Even though we can't change anything ourselves for the moment, we have to convey our messages.' Juan Luis Guerra and his 4.40 group are perhaps the oxygen that our Latin dance music needs in these times of creative crisis.

## Sounds from Colombia

So, leaving sentimental salsa aside, there have been quite a few interesting innovations from which dancers have been able to profit in recent years. Colombia has seen the most important of these. The media's obssession with cocaine has concealed the fact that Colombia is now the second exporter of salsa music after Puerto Rico. This salsa is steeped in the folklore of our Pacific and Caribbean coasts. Of course, there have been plenty of critics who have linked the rise in the number of these bands – there are at least fifty in Cali, for example – with the laundering of money from cocaine trafficking.

Salsa lovers of all ages have turned to Colombia for signs of renovation in the music, especially with the cumbia, which also has its roots in African music. Colombian bands are now so good at salsa that few foreign bands are ever contracted to play there. Moreover, many of the Colombian bands tour Europe and the United States themselves.

Colombia is a country where the people dance for any reason and on any occasion, so it was bound to produce groups like these. It is no coincidence that the cumbia, from the Caribbean region, is the national dance, and in the south of Latin America is even more popular than salsa itself. In the 1970s Fruko y sus Tesos appeared, adapting New York rhythms to the urban realities of their own country. One of Fruko's songs in particular was sung on every street corner throughout the continent, until it became a huge hit, and led to Fruko being invited to the annual Fania Allstars concert.

*En el mundo en que yo vivo*
*siempre hay cuatro esquinas,*
*pero entre esquina y esquina*
*siempre habrá lo mismo.*

*Para mí no existe el cielo,*
*ni luna ni estrellas*
*pa'mí no existe el sol,*
*pa'mí todo es tinieblas...*

*Condenado para siempre en esta horrible celda*
*donde no llega el cariño ni la voz de nadie*
*aquí me paso los días y la noche entera*
*sólo vivo del recuerdo eterno de mi madre...*

The world I live in
always has four corners,
but between corner and corner
nothing ever changes.

For me there is no sky
or moon or stars
for me there is no sun
for me shadows are everywhere.

Condemned forever to this dreadful cell
where there's no affection, or anyone else's voice
here I spend all my days and nights
living only thanks to the eternal memory of my mother...

*El preso*, version by Fruko y sus Tesos

For several years, Fruko was Colombia's leading salsa singer. Apart from him there were only a few bands that ever became known outside Colombia. It was only in the early 1990s that a new group which combined the current salsa sound with the musical and oral traditions of the Colombian Pacific coast emerged to offer something new to salsa dancers. This group, Niche, appeared just at the moment when the possibilities of salsa in New York appeared to have been exhausted, giving them the chance to present something new and make their name. They were followed by La Verdad, a group led by a former singer from Fruko, Joe Arroyo, who managed to combine elements from salsa, the Caribbean, and Colombian folklore in a highly professional way.

It was Niche which drew international attention to a phenomenon that had existed since the 1960s: namely the worship of salsa in the cities of Cali and Barranquilla. The inhabitants of the latter city, on the Caribbean coast, claimed they were the owners of salsa, while the people of Cali, close to the Pacific, insist salsa belongs to them. Cali's inhabitants are also the greatest appreciators of the pachanga and Ricardo Ray. Since the late 1960s, people in Cali have been heard to boast that 'Puerto Rico and New York may play it, but Cali dances it.'

It is difficult to argue with that assertion. For three consecutive years in the mid 1970s dancers from Cali won the first three places in the world salsa championship held in New York, until they were eventually excluded from the competition. To end all argument, people from Cali also point out that almost every group has dedicated a song to their city; and that their local university is the only one in the world to offer courses and seminars on the history and instruments of salsa music. Salsa as it is danced in Cali is traditional, untouched by the eighties fashions, unlike any other. It incorporates elements from the black Caribbean, from the tango and from rock and roll; it's acrobatic, speedy, and the role played by the woman is crucial.

But the people of Cali and Barranquilla are not the only Colombians to enjoy salsa dancing. Take the youth of Medellín's slum neighbourhoods. In this conservative, hardworking city, the mambo was banned because it was considered too vulgar. But in the hillside slums around the centre of the city, salsa has acquired a special significance. As in so many other cities of our continent, Caribbean music reached Medellín through prostitution. It is only in recent years that salsa has been widely accepted. Two factors are responsible for this. Firstly, a new generation of university students and intellectuals broke with long-held prejudices and saw Colombia's second city as a single entity. Secondly, many youngsters turned to working directly or indirectly with the cocaine traffickers, because of the few possibilities for earning an honest living. These young people found their philosophical identity in salsa. Something similar has occurred with the young criminals in Lima, Guayaquil, Caracas, and other cities on the continent.

For these youngsters, salsa offers the promise that they can live life to the full for today, and welcome death as something to celebrate.[8] Some of them adopted the following salsa song as their anthem, to be sung even at their funerals:

*Hay que pasar la vida siempre alegre*
*después que uno se muere de qué vale,*
*hay que gozar de todos los placeres*
*cuando uno va a morir, nadie lo sabe.*

*Como la vida es corta yo la vivo*
*y gozo con el vino y las mujeres,*
*he de pasar mi vida siempre alegre.*
*No quiero que me llores cuando muera*
*si tienes que llorar, llórame en vida*
*así yo puedo ver si hay quién me quiera*
*o quién me va engañando con mentiras...*

*(coro)*
*Vive la vida,*
*mira que se va y no vuelve...*

Always be happy in your life
after you're dead what's the point
you have to enjoy every pleasure
who knows when death may strike.

Life is short but I mean to live it
enjoying wine and women,
I intend to be happy always.
I don't want any tears when I die
cry while I'm alive if you want to

so I can see who cares for me
and who is fooling me with lies...

(chorus)
Live your life
it's passing, and never comes back...

*Siempre alegre*, version by Raphy Leavit


Having said this, salsa is not a music simply for delinquents – a small minority among its devotees – nor does it incite criminality. Everyone accepts and enjoys it in their own way. For example, looking at the song above, some people are only interested in the lines: 'I don't want any tears when I die/cry while I'm alive if you want to...' and spend whole days humming it, sometimes wife to husband, sometimes the other way round. And how many control freaks should heed the words of the chorus?

That's why it's important to remember these lines from various salsa songs: 'Enjoy the dance, forget what race you're from, when you're dancing, there's no such thing as colour, dance all together whether it's hot or cold. Brown hair, blond or black look the same when you're dancing salsa, which makes the world happy. Dance, be happy, don't be sad, what's needed in this world is more fun to bring us together.'

*Cuando me piden que les toque rumba*
*se vuelven locos;*
*y cuando suena mi recio tumbao*
*les tiembla el alma,*
*se les moja la ropa en sudor*
*y se empapan la conciencia*
*del sonido percusivo;*
*es que quieren su vida acabar*
*enajenados de emoción*
*con esa mágica y sonora polirítmia*
*que les quebranta la razón.*

*Cuando me pongo a sonar los cueros de mi tambor*
*la gente corre a bailar porque la rumba soy yo.*

When they ask me to play rumba
they all go crazy;
and when they hear the beat of my drum
their souls start to tremble,
their clothes are dripping with sweat
and their mind is soaked through
with the incessant beat;
they'd be happy to die
from so much emotion
the magical rhythms
drive them completely wild.

When I start to play the skin of my drum
everyone runs to dance because I am the rumba.

*La rumba soy yo*, version by La Sonora Ponceña

## Salsa comes of age

The tango singer Carlos Gardel once sang a line that no prisoner can bear to hear: 'Twenty years are nothing.' It could be said that salsa itself has been in existence for over twenty years, with all its merits and defects. But its flavours, as we have seen, have been brewing for five hundred years: it is multiracial, multicultural, multimelodic, multirhythmic. So it's not surprising that there should now be House-salsa or Rap-salsa, or even the Orquesta de la Luz, which consists entirely of Japanese musicians. It's true that their female singer has some problems with her Spanish, which makes it hard for her to improvise or develop the art of soneo, which all salsa maestros are supposed to have. But we Latins should feel proud that people so culturally different from ourselves should honour us with such respect, and take it so seriously. The same could be said of Europe, where nearly every country now has its salsa bands.

To end, I return to the words of Héctor Lavoe, who passed away recently: 'lend me a few hours of your life. If this night is lost, let's at least find each other'; and to Ismael Rivera, sadly no longer with us either: 'the sea smashed my house down/but I liked the sound, so I built it again'; and finally, Ruben Blades: 'it all depends on the way you look at things...'

That's salsa. Irreverent freedom.

# NOTES

## Chapter 1

1. Eduardo Galeano, *The Open Veins of Latin America*, Monthly Review Press, New York, 1973

2. Claude Fleouter, *La mémoire du peuple noir*, Editions Albin Michel, Paris, 1979

3. León Argeliers, *Del canto y el tiempo*, Editorial Letras Cubanas, Havana, 1984

4. Fernando Ortiz, *Los bailes y el teatro de los negros en el folklor de Cuba*, Editorial Letras Cubanas, Havana, 1985

5. *ibid*

6. *ibid*

7. Argeliers, *Del canto y el tiempo*

8. César Pagano, 'Salsa: Ritmo y libertad', Colombia, unpublished paper

9. 'What's Cuba playing at?' Co-production BBC TV and Cuban TV, 1988

10. Argeliers, *Del canto y el tiempo*

11. Fernando Ortiz, *La africanía de la música folklórica de Cuba*, Editora Universitaria, Cuba, 1965

12. Argeliers, *Del canto y el tiempo*

13. Félix Solono, 'El danzón y su inventor, Miguel Failde', article published in *Cuba Musical*, Havana, 1928

## Chapter 2

1. Argeliers, *Del canto y el tiempo*

2. Helio Orovio, *Diccionario de la música cubana*, Editorial Letras Cubanas, Havana, 1981

3. Luís Martínez Rovira, 'De Cienfuegos te traigo un son', in *Revista Bohemia*, Cuba, 1984

4. *Ibid*

5. Carlos Serna and Marcos Barro, *La Sonora Matancera, más de 60 años de historia musical*, Editorial Ediciones Fuentes, Colombia 1990

6. 'What's Cuba playing at?' BBC TV/Cuban TV, 1988

7. Interview with Rafael Lay by Brena Hernández, 1981

8. Hugo Chaparro Valderrama, 'Hoy como ayer', in *Magazín Dominical*, Colombia

9. Enrique Sánchez Hernani, 'Beny Moré, Canto desde lejos', in *La República*, June 1986, Peru

# Chapter 3

1. Pedro Malavet, *Del bolero a la nueva canción*, Puerto Rico, 1988

2. Claude Fleouter, *La mémoire du peuple noir*, Editions Albin Michel, Paris, 1979

3. Héctor Manuel Colón. 'La calle que les marxistas nunca entendieron', paper presented in the symposium, 'Puerto Rico Today', National Autonomous University (UNAM), Mexico, 1983

4. Fleouter, *La mémoire du peuple noir*

5. Charles Delaunay,'El Jazz y la cultura mundial'

6. Jacques B Hess, 'Be-bop Jazz Hot' Enciclopedie L'Instante, Paris, 1989

7. Rafael Quintero and Rafael Bassi, 'La salsa de concierto', Paper read as part of the conference 'Salsa, música de América Latina', Universidad del Valle, Cali, Colombia, June 1984

8. Enrique Sánchez Hernani, 'Ritmo y Catarsis' in *La República*, Peru, 9.2.86

9. Quintero and Bassi, *'La salsa de concierto'*

10. Malavet, *Del bolero a la nueva canción*

11. César Miguel Rondón, *El libro de la salsa*, Caracas, 1980

12. 'Ismael Rivera, retrato de boricua', Film made by the Instituto Cultural de Puerto Rico

13. Edgardo Rodríguez, *El entierro de Cortijo*, Ediciones Huracán, Puerto Rico, 1988

14. César Miguel Rondón, Interview with Ismael Rivera, in *El libro de la salsa*

# Chapter 4

1. Interview with the pianist Alfredo Rodríguez, May 1991

2. César Miguel Rondón, *El libro de la salsa*

3. Héctor Manuel Colón. 'La calle que les marxistas nunca entendieron'

4. José Artega, *La Salsa*, Intermedio Editores, Colombia 1990

# Chapter 5

1. César Miguel Rondón, *El libro de la salsa*

2. Extract from a letter by Willie Colón to the author, 21.11.91

## Chapter 6

1. Interview with Alfredo de la Fé carried out by Jimmy Abdala Oliveros, Colombia, 1991

2. Fania's film, 'Salsa' is not to be confused with a film of the same name made by Boaz Davidson in 1988. Davidson's film portrayed salsa as an epileptic form of disco music and Puerto Ricans as a bunch of layabouts.

## Chapter 7

1. Mariela Quintero Rivera, 'East Harlem Music School: Sonidos de alegría y esperanza', in *Rojo* magazine, Puerto Rico, June 1990

2. Umberto Valverde, *Celia Cruz, Reina Rumba*, Colombia 1981

3. César Miguel Rondón, *El libro de la salsa*

4. Celia Cruz quoted by Pilar Nuñez Carvallo, in the magazine *QueHacer*, Peru 1989

5. Papo Lucca interviewed by the author, June 1991

## Chapter 8

1. Congressional Record. Proceedings and debates of the 102nd Congress, first session, Washington, 8.1.91

## Chapter 9

1. Luis Aparicio Delgado, in the magazine *Oiga*, January 1990, Peru

2. The journalist, Jaime Torres wrote three detailed articles for the Puerto Rican *El Nuevo Día* in July 1988, in which he revealed the existence of irregular promotion practices in the media, particularly radio. Payment was either by bribes to individual DJs, through sexual favours or costly presents.

3. From interviews with the timbal player Willie Rosario and the singer Cheo Feliciano by Yves Billón, July 1991

4. The magazine *La Clave* from Puerto Rico, issue No.1, Sept-Oct. 1988 contains valuable analyses of this issue.

5. The pianist Alfredo Rodríguez interviewed by the author, May 1991

6. Interview with the violinist Alfredo De La Fé by Jimmy Abdala Oliveros, June 1991

7. *Escala*, 21.4.91, Dominican Republic

8. Alonso Salazar, *Born to die in Medellín*, Latin America Bureau, London, 1993

# GLOSSARY

From the moment that the black slaves had to conceal the worship of their gods because of persecution from the colonial government and the Catholic church, words and meanings were created or changed. Almost simultaneously, the cultural mixing that occurred meant these expressions acquired a new richness and not only became part of music and other expressions of culture, but of daily life as well. The continuing development of what could be called Afro-Cuban, Afro-Caribbean or Afro-Latin music, always on the limit of the permissible, or simply involving different social or political circumstances, has given rise to a very special 'superSpanish'. Although the terms may vary from region to region, these are the main ones; also included are some usages from the practice of santería.

Achantado: humiliated, depressed. Thought to be derived from the proud members of the Ashanti community from West Africa, who escaped oppression by throwing themselves from the slave ships or by hanging themselves in the slave huts, rather than accept their condition as slaves.

Aché or ashé: invocation of the gods. The supernatural power conferred by the orishas on their children and on the objects associated with worship of them. Also used as a greeting, with the meaning: 'good luck and health to all my brothers'.

Allstars: musical group formed for a special event from the best instrumentalists and singers of other groups.

Anacaona: indigenous chief. Wife of the leader Caonabo on the island of Hispaniola (today Haiti and the Dominican Republic). Fought the Spaniards with her husband, and was hanged on the orders of Fray Nicolas de Ovando, governor of the island.

Arará: Afro-Cuban cult practised by slaves who came from the Dahomey region in Africa.

Babalao: priest in the Lucumí religion.

Babalú ayé: African god. God of illnesses. In the synchretism of santería, Saint Lazarus.

Bacalao: loose liver; someone with deceitful ways: 'I recognise you bacalao, even though you're in disguise'.

Bacán or bacana: a good man: wholesome, refined, generous, happy, noble.

Bailes de cuna: celebrations held in the last century in houses in the poor quarters of Cuban towns, to which young people from rich families went in order to dance the contradanza.

Barrancón: hut where the slaves slept on the sugar plantations.

El Barrio: Neighbourhood, district of a town. In New York, 'El Barrio' was the name given to Latin districts in the Bronx and Harlem, where Latins have concentrated since the 1940s, taking with them the way of life of Latin American cities. Musicians in the Barrio were the first to create salsa.

Batá: set of three sacred drums used in Yoruba rituals to communicate with the orishas, their gods, when played by the olobata drummers in a state of possession.

Bemba: having a big mouth, or protruding lips: 'you've got a scarlet mouth'; 'the fatlipped black'.

Bembé: in the past, a ritual with drums in honour of a Yoruba god. Nowadays, a popular celebration: 'How's the bembé going?'

Big Bands/Jazz Band Cubana: original name for the big Cuban dance bands which had adopted the saxophone from jazz bands.

Bochinche: real or imaginary stories from popular neighbourhoods, passed on by word of mouth. The people named in them are often unaware of their existence.

La Bomba: traditional Puerto Rican rhythm.

Bongo: percussion instrument of African origin created in Cuba. It consists of two small drums joined by a length of wood, and produces a highpitched sound. Held between the knees and played with the fingers and the palms of the hands.

Borinquen: an affectionate term for Puerto Rico.

Bossa nova: Brazilian rumba rhythm which became very popular in the 1960s.

Bungas: originally the clay pots that oil was carried in. Later used to describe the musical groups in the east of Cuba which combined African and Spanish music to produce the son.

Cencerro or Campana: metal instrument like a cowbell, played with a wooden stick.

Chachacha: one of the best known Cuban rhythms, and one of the easiest. A traditional dance rhythm based on the danzón, made popular by the charanga groups.

Changó: African divinity. God of fire, of thunder, and of virility. In the synchretic practices of santería, Changó is Saint Barbara in Cuba and Saint Jerome in Brazil.

Charanga: musical group based around the flute and violins. First appeared in the 18th century, due to French influences.

La Clave: musical instrument. Two round wooden sticks about a foot long. Usually held by the singer or chorus, and struck together to keep the beat: three beats, pause, two beats.

Combo: musical group with an average of eight to ten musicians.

Conga or tumbadores (more rarely, mambisa): fundamental drum in Cuban popular music. Played with the hand, combining percussion and stroking.

Conjunto: name for the musical groups which played the son. Usually included: trumpets, piano, tres, double-bass, congas, bongo, guiro, maracas, and clave.

Cuatro: guitar with four double strings, used principally in Puerto Rico.

Descarga: free musical improvisation. A way of playing taken from the jazz bands and adapted to Cuban music. Much used in salsa music, where each tune includes a freestyle section, played on all the percussion instruments.

Espanglish or Spanglish: the term for the mixture of 'poor Spanish and worse English' that some Latins in the US speak.

Gringos: Latin American slang for North Americans.

Guaguancó: Cuban rhythm originating among the African black slaves. An improvised song accompanied by three drums played by hand. The most popular urban dance, performed with a partner.

Guajiro(a): Cuban peasant.

Guajira: music of the Cuban countryside strongly influenced by Spanish traditions, notably in the 'tres' guitars and the oral romance tradition which was used to describe the peasants' daily life; claves, maracas and the güiro were also used.

Guapo: a man to fear; someone ready for a fight, fearless; can also be used to denote a handsome, welldressed man.

Guateque: Afro-Cuban dance. Noisy meeting of popular classes.

Guayaberas: highly-coloured puffed sleeved shirts worn by some musical groups; a typical example of Mexican tropicalism in Caribbean folklore.

Güiro: musical instrument made from a gourd. The contents of the gourd are scooped out, and the gourd is dried. A series of wide or narrow vertical grooves are cut into the skin; held in the left hand and scraped with a drumstick.

Jibara: Puerto Rican country music.

Jibaro: nowadays, generic term for a Puerto Rican. Not to be confused with the term for a drug pusher.

Latin-jazz: term used for Afro-Cuban rhythms played by jazz bands which have a Cuban percussion section.

Malandro, malandrín: neighbourhood gangster, usually noticeable for his smart appearance.

Mambi: from the Congo root 'mbi', signifying evil, cruel, savage; by extension powerful, fearful. Used by the blacks who fought for their freedom. Afterwards it became a term of great patriotic honour, like the 'sans culottes' in France.

Mambo: originally, santero priest. Later used for the rhythm created in Cuba by Orestes López, and developed by Dámaso Perez Prado. Also used for the simultaneous entry of instruments in the middle or just before the end of a piece, especially when the saxophones play across the trumpets.

Maracas: musical instrument made from small dried gourds. Seeds, stones or bits of metal are put inside, and a stick is added to hold them with. Nowadays made from all kinds of material, such as plastic or leather.

Marímbula: African hand piano. Made from a wooden box with metal strips for keys.

Montuno: a word deriving originally from 'monte', meaning the countryside, particularly in the east of Cuba. In the 1920s-1930s, the son groups began to use a second section called montuno in their arrangements, in which the melody gave way to the rhythm. Nowadays, this section is very important in many arrangements.

Niche: negro.

Niuyorrican: used for the children of Puerto Ricans born in New York.

Niuyorlatin: used for children of Latin Americans born in New York.

Obatalá: African goddess of creativity. In santería synchretism, identified with Our Lady of Mercy.

Ochún: African divinity. Goddess of rivers and of love. In santería, represents Our Lady of the Caridad del Cobre.

Ogún: African divinity. God of metals and of war. In santería, represents Saint Peter.

Olofí: supreme god of the Yoruba cult.

Orishas: African divinities or powers.

Orquesta Típica: charanga groups which played rhythms like the danzón or the chachacha.

Pachanga: rhythm with African roots, played in New York around the mid-1960s.

La Plena: typical rhythm from Puerto Rico.

Pregón: the term used in Cuba for street sellers crying their wares; also used for musicians singing in the street.

Quisqueya: from the Dominican Republic.

Rumba: during colonial times in Cuba, a kind of popular rhythm and dance with African influences. Later the term came to be used to describe various musical rhythms produced in Cuba. Nowadays, a celebration where salsa music is played.

Rumbero: a person who needs to dance to live.

Rumbiar: to dance.

Salsero(a): a salsa lover.

Salsoteca: place with a valuable collection of salsa and Afro-Caribbean music.

Sambia: supreme god of the congo rites.

Sandunga: apparently derived from the Andalucian term 'sa' meaning 'salt cellar' and 'ndungu', the African word for black pepper. Salt and pepper are the twin symbols of Cuban music.

Santería: a word of Yoruba origin, signifying the most important of the Afro-Cuban-Catholic rites. The rites in which the African divinities are integrated with the Catholic god and saints.

Santero: priest in the Santería rites.

Saoco: taste. The taste to be able to play Caribbean music.

Siete Potencias Africanas: the seven most important African divinities: Olofí, Obatalá, Yemayá, Changó, Ochún, Ogún, and Babalú Aye.

Son: typically Cuban kind of dance music, developed in the 19th and early 20th centuries, which balances European and African musical influences. The son provided salsa with rhythmic and harmonic models.

Soneo: difficult art that every good singer of Afro-Cuban-Latin dance music must have. Includes a sense of rhythm, a gift for improvisation, perfect pitch, and individual style, which enables the singer to lead and interact with choruses and instruments.

Sonero: singer who has the gift of soneo.

Swing: rhythmic quality of jazz, especially prominent between 1940-1945; later applied to any strong, successful intepretation of Afro-Cuban-Latin music: 'a rhythm with swing'.

Timbales: drums on a tripod, with a cylindrical metal base, played with drumsticks. Usually accompanied by two bells, one larger than the other.

Tiple: soft-sounding guitar, mainly associated today with traditional Colombian music.

Tirar paso or marcar paso: to dance.

Tres: guitar with three double strings, found in Cuba.

Tumbadoras: cylindrical drums about a metre high, with a taut goatskin across the top to provide sound. Introduced into son music by Arsenio Rodríguez at the end of the 1930s.

Vacunao: sudden movement of a dancer in the guaguancó, in which symbolic sexual contact is made with the partner.

Yemayá: African divinity. Goddess of the sea and of motherhood. In santería represents the Christian Our Lady of Regla (order).

Yores, Yores Estaites: New York.

Zapateo: Cuban country dance with Spanish influence, involving frequent leaps, common in the 18th and 19th centuries.

# INDEX

146

# BOOKS FROM THE LATIN AMERICA BUREAU

## AFROCUBA
### An Anthology of Cuban Writing on Race, Politics and Culture

#### Pedro Pérez Sarduy & Jean Stubbs (eds)

What is it like to be black in Cuba? Does racism exist in a revolutionary society which claims to have abolished it? How does the legacy of slavery and segregation live on in today's Cuba?

**AfroCuba** looks at the black experience in Cuba through the eyes of the island's writers, scholars and artists. Writings - poetry, fiction, political analysis and anthropology - from over thirty, mainly black, contributors give a multi-faceted insight into Cuba's rich ethnic and cultural reality.

*'This first comprehensive compilation of an AfroCuban identity is as readable as it is original.'* **New Statesman and Society**

310 pages, with index     1993     ISBN 0 906156 75 0 (pbk)     £12.99
Distributed in the USA by the Talman Company, New York


## FACES OF LATIN AMERICA
### Duncan Green

From Argentina to Venezuela, a bestselling exploration of the people and processes which have shaped modern Latin America. **Faces of Latin America** celebrates the vibrant culture of its peoples and looks at key actors in the region's turbulent politics with chapters on the military, democracy, the guerrillas, indigenous peoples, the Church and the women's movement.

*'An indispensable introduction and source of reference.'* **New Statesman and Society**

224 pages, with photos and index     1991     ISBN 0 906156 59 9 (pbk)     £8.99


## BORN TO DIE IN MEDELLIN
### Alonso Salazar

The world of youth gangs in Colombia's second city, illuminated with testimony from the teenagers themselves. 'A lively, detailed and authentic first-hand account of life - or more usually death - at the sharp end of the drug war in Colombia.' **The Independent on Sunday**

144 pages     1992     ISBN 0 906156 66 1 (pbk)     £5.99

# IN FOCUS
## People * Politics * Culture

IN FOCUS guides to the countries of Latin America and the Caribbean cover issues that other guides don't. Each 80-page guide, illustrated with colour photos, looks at:

* Culture: what makes the country distinctive, its traditions and modern influences, music, media and sport

* Politics: the key actors in the system, parties, social movements, elections

* Society: rich and poor, women and their role, town and country, health and education, migration and development

* History: the presence of the past, colonialism and independence, heroes and villains, war and peace

All guides have a 'key facts and figures' section and foldout map.

## CUBA IN FOCUS

Cuba is in crisis. After thirty five years of one-party rule, the island stands on the brink of dramatic change. Its economy destroyed by the collapse of the eastern bloc, its people suffering increased hardship, Cuba's unique political and social structures are close to collapse. What is life like in Cuba at this decisive moment in its history?

June 1995      ISBN 0 906156 95 5 (pbk)      £5.99

## VENEZUELA IN FOCUS

For 35 years Venezuela enjoyed its reputation as Latin America's richest and most democratic nation with, during the 1970s, an extraordinary oil boom which changed the face of the country. Yet since 1990, the oil bonanza has been replaced by austerity and violence, shaking Venezuela's peaceful image and creating a deep social crisis. Despite its economic and political problems, Venezuela is also a country of spectacular natural beauty and cultural richness.

October 1994     ISBN 0 906156 92 0 (pbk)      £5.99

## JAMAICA IN FOCUS

Jamaica is a complex, vibrant and often violent society; a country beset with widespread poverty, political instability and crime. But Jamaica is also the scene of intense cultural activity, a place where music, poetry and religion colour everyday life. Synonymous with reggae music, Jamaica reflects its mixed ethnic and cultural heritage in many artistic forms.

October 1993     ISBN 0 906156 81 5 (pbk)      £5.99

# BOLIVIA IN FOCUS

Bolivia is a country full of rich traditions stemming from before the arrival of Columbus. In this most Indian of Latin American nations, pre-Conquest lifestyles, languages and dress have adapted to survive centuries of oppression and forced labour in silver and tin mines which dot the landscape.

August 1994                    ISBN 0 906156 91 2 (pbk)                    £5.99

# REBEL RADIO
## The story of El Salvador's Radio Venceremos
### José Ignacio López Vigil

El Salvador. The civil war. The guerrillas need a radio station to win hearts and minds. Radio Venceremos. An underground station that keeps broadcasting whatever the cost - under helicopter attack, against high-tech jamming, on the run from endless army offensives.

Fast-moving, in turn funny and tragic, **Rebel Radio** is about history in the making as the men and women of Radio Venceremos relive their war.

*'These remarkable stories tell a tale of almost incredible courage and ingenuity in the struggle to keep the spark of hope alive in a country being turned into a living Hell. It is a real tribute to the human spirit.'*
Noam Chomsky, author of **Turning the Tide: US Intervention in Central America**

*'The work of Radio Venceremos is legendary and the stories of how it became so are rich in humanity, wit and, above all, heroism.'*
John Pilger, award-winning filmmaker and author of **Heroes** and **Distant Voices**

*'An exciting tale filled with political intrigue, youthful hi-jinks, passionate love and clandestine sexual liaisons in the mountains of Morazán.'*
Robert Armstrong, co-author with Janet Shenk of **El Salvador: The Face of Revolution**

José Ignacio López Vigil is a broadcaster, writer of radio soap operas and author of books on radical radio in Bolivia and Nicaragua. Based in Lima, Peru, he is the Latin American representative of the World Association of Community Radio Broadcasters.

256 pages            April 1995            ISBN 0 906156 88 2 (pbk)            £8.99

First published in Spanish by UCA Editores, San Salvador
Published in the USA by Curbstone Press

# ON THE LINE
## Life on the US-Mexican Border
### Augusta Dwyer

First and third worlds meet on the US-Mexican border. A point of entry for impoverished Mexicans, it is also the location for 2,000 foreign-owned assembly plants employing 500,000 low-paid workers - most of them women.

To write **On The Line**, Augusta Dwyer travelled the length of the border, uncovering the stories of ordinary Mexicans - workers in the *maquiladora* assembly plants, illegal migrants, border guards, and environmentalists. Her journey through the crowded, dirty border towns reveals the true costs of free trade.

152 pages, index        1994            ISBN 0 906156 84 X (pbk)            £8.99

# THE LATIN AMERICAN CITY
## Alan Gilbert

In all but five Latin American countries, more people now live in towns and cities than in the countryside. **The Latin American City** surveys the region's urban explosion since the 1950s from the perspective of the poor.

It asks why people are attracted to the city and examines the underlying problems of rural poverty which fuels the exodus. It explores the options open to those arriving in the city and the strategies for acquiring land and building a home.

*'A thorough introduction for the non-specialist and a useful survey for students of Latin American Studies.'* **British Bulletin of Publications.**

192 pages, with photos and index        1994        ISBN 0 906156 82 3 (pbk)        £8.99

**To order Latin America Bureau books by post, please add 10% to cover prices (20% for overseas, surface mail) for post and packing.**

**Orders to: Latin America Bureau, 1 Amwell Street, London EC1R 1UL**

**and for US orders  to: Monthly Review Press, 122 West 27 Street, New York NY 10001 USA**

**LAB Books are also available from:**

Trocaire Resource Centre, 12 Cathedral Street, Dublin 1 Ireland

Lateinamerika Nachrichten, Gneisenaustr 2, 10961 Berlin 61 Germany

Solidarity House, Fredensborgveien 37, 0177 Oslo, Norway

E R Ruward BV Spui 231 2511 BP Den Haag, Netherlands

# FREE CD/CASSETTE OFFER
*You've read the book, now hear the music!*

JUST FILL IN THE VOUCHER BELOW AND SEND IT TO THE LATIN
AMERICA BUREAU IN LONDON.

## *Voucher valid in the UK AND EUROPE ONLY*

The Latin America Bureau and TUMI Music offer you a *free* salsa album, *Tropical Extravaganza*. This album is an excellent introduction to some of the salsa and Caribbean dance music introduced in *Salsa: Havana Heat, Bronx Beat*. Capturing the magic of a Caribbean dance party, the album combines a rich mix of Latin America's top salsa and cumbia performers with the hottest tropical rhythms. Featured bands include Cuba's La Sonora Matancera and Colombia's Los Alfa 8.

## TUMI MUSIC LTD
8-9 New Bond St Place, Bath, Avon BA1 1BH, UK. Tel 01225 462367

*Tropical Extravaganza* is just one of 40 albums on the Tumi Music label. Tumi strives to protect indigenous Latin American culture and traditions by bringing them to a wider international audience. The company's albums range from the haunting pan-pipe music of the Andes to vibrant salsa of the Caribbean tropics.

*For a free TUMI Music catalogue, tick box below or contact TUMI direct.*

✂ - - - - - - - - - - - - - - - - - - - - - - - - - - - - - - - - - - - - - - - - - - - - - - - - - - - - - - - - -

## FREE CD/CASSETTE VOUCHER
### (*valid in the UK and Europe* only)

Send to: LAB, 1 Amwell St, London EC1R 1UL, UK.
Please send me *Tropical Extravaganza* in:

☐ CD format  ☐ cassette format  (tick *one* box only)

Please send me a free Tumi music catalogue ☐

Name ................................................................................................

Address................................................................................................

................................................................Postcode ......................